Subject Access to a Multilingual Museum Database

Recent Titles in Libraries Unlimited
Third Millennium Cataloging Series

Sheila Intner and Susan Lazinger, Series Editors

Using the Open Archives Initiative Protocol for Metadata Harvesting
Timothy W. Cole and Muriel Foulonneau

Subject Access to a Multilingual Museum Database

A Step-by-Step Approach to the Digitization Process

Dr. Allison Siffre Guedalia Kupietzky

Third Millennium Cataloging
Susan Lazinger and Sheila Intner, Series Editors

A Member of the Greenwood Publishing Group

Westport, Connecticut • London

Library of Congress Cataloging-in-Publication Data

Kupietzky, Allison Siffre Guedalia, 1965–
    Subject access to a multilingual museum database : a step-by-step approach to the digitization process / Allison Siffre Guedalia Kupietzky.
        p. cm. — (Third millennium cataloging)
    Includes bibliographical references and index.
    ISBN-13: 978-1-59158-444-5 (alk. paper)
    1. Museums—Data processing. 2. Muze'on Yisra'el (Jerusalem)—Data processing. 3. Muze'on Yisra'el (Jerusalem)—Management. 4. Museums—Collection management—Digitization. 5. Cross-language information retrieval. 6. Museums—Management. I. Title.
    AM139.K87   2007
    069.0285—dc22   2007013543

British Library Cataloguing in Publication Data is available.

Library of Congress Catalog Card Number: 2007013543
ISBN-13: 978-1-59158-444-5

First published in 2007

Libraries Unlimited, 88 Post Road West, Westport, CT 06881
A Member of the Greenwood Publishing Group, Inc.
www.lu.com

Printed in the United States of America

The paper used in this book complies with the Permanent Paper Standard issued by the National Information Standards Organization (Z39.48–1984).

10   9   8   7   6   5   4   3   2   1

Contents

List of Illustrations

FIGURES

TABLES

Preface

ABSTRACT

In the world of museums, it is the management of holdings that allows a museum to fulfill its pedagogic and preservation missions. A museum that can gear its cataloguing for the easiest and most comprehensive access will enable its curators, researchers, and the public to interact with and gain the most from these objets d'art. This book includes a comprehensive study of museum computerization systems, that is, what is available, what is used worldwide, pitfalls and successes, a case study of the computerization process of a museum's collection, and is arranged in a didactic manner for training the reader to become a collections database manager. It contains the "whos, whats, wheres, whys, and hows" of choosing and implementing the right computer system to manage museums' holdings, with specific emphasis on how to accomplish this in a multilingual setting.

This book is comprised of two elements: theory and application. The theory concerns computerization of mono- or multilingual museums worldwide and the application of this to a multilingual museum and its database. Part I includes a review of the problems and of the literature concerning computerization methods used in the computerization of museums.

Part II includes guidelines for mono- or multilingual museums seeking to implement a database system to aid in cataloguing its holdings. In order to apply these ideas to all museums, a six-step process of computerizing museum collections called the SAGE-K method was developed to facilitate the application of these ideas by all museums and enable them to achieve the goal of digitization.

INTRODUCTION

Digitization is being used in many different disciplines. This book deals specifically with the challenges and problems involved in digitization of collections found in the museum setting. Many museums have already tried digitizing and have encountered problems. This book aims to share the experiences of some of these museums by compiling helpful advice. Museums have used the groundwork of the library world as a springboard for the development of their collections management systems, yet there are many differences between the disciplines.

When the author was first asked to contribute to the *Third Millennium Cataloging Series*, it was felt that it would be crucial at the onset to define the differences between museums, libraries, and archives. While all three types of institutions place a great emphasis on cataloguing their collections, libraries are one hundred years ahead of museums in their cataloguing efforts and, as a result, have achieved greater standardization. This success in standardization lies not only in the libraries' years of experience but also in the material being catalogued—books.

When a book is published it appears in many copies. This means that no one book is unique. The book appears with a list of attributes that are objective in their description: the author, title, publisher, and year all appear printed on the book (in most cases) and leave little room for subjective speculation. As soon as one library catalogues the book, any library can copy its cataloguing and apply it to its own library. Of course libraries also catalogue many other types of materials: maps, videos, Web sites, doctoral dissertations, and manuscripts, and bibliographic records for these materials often need special fields. Yet there is still a level of objectivity in this cataloguing process. Each library relates to the attributes of its collections in a similar manner, except for the subject access field. Although there is an ongoing attempt to standardize subject headings—within the library community there is widespread use of Library of Congress Subject Headings (LCSH) worldwide—there is some customization, or subjectivity, in the cataloguing of the subject access fields. The title of this book, *Subject Access*, refers to this unique set of fields, which identifies a book in relation to its intended readers. The same book, for example, Leonardo's sketchbook of the human form, might receive the subject access field "anatomy" in the science library and the subject access field "drawing" in the art library.

An object from a museum collection is unique. Even if the same mold is used to create a series of sculptures, each object has its own provenance (history of ownership), exhibition history, and markings. This one-of-a-kind distinctiveness is manifested in the cataloguing process, as a curator catalogues a museum item in specialized fields reflecting the medium, time period, and creator of the item. Much of the information registered when cataloguing a sculpture in one museum cannot be copied and applied to a sculpture from another museum. The attributes of the object and their most basic descriptors are often speculative or subjective. For example, artist name, year of production, and place of origin usually do not appear alongside the object in its inception as with a book but rather require the curators to research them and come to their own conclusions. This subjective descriptive method leads to different information on exactly the same object.

Another basic difference between the book and the museum object is that the book in its essence is tied to a language. On the other hand, a museum object has no linguistic source. The cataloguing of the object is not tied to any one language, and the content of the work of art transcends geographic or linguistic borders. For this reason within the museum world there is often a need for a truly bilingual or multilingual environment. Each object should be accessible in any language so as to be appreciated visually by a worldwide audience.

An archives, as opposed to libraries, collects original unpublished material or primary sources. The records held by archives are unique and irreplaceable. By their very nature archival materials are fragile and vulnerable to improper handling. If an archival document is lost, stolen, or irreparably damaged, the information it contains is lost forever. While libraries collect published material, also known as secondary sources, the unique nature of archival material has led archives to develop stringent security procedures. Researchers cannot browse through the stacks as they do in a library, and archival material can only be consulted in supervised reading rooms.

As a result of dealing with primary sources, an archives must catalogue the material using subjective descriptive texts and individual cataloguing fields. Although there are differences between the library and an archives, the similarity of the material rests in its textual format. The great difference between museums and archives lies in the importance of visual documentation. At present in the museum world, it is critical to have a visual manifestation of the object (the Ministry of Education's Department of Museums in Israel requires that all catalogued objects be photographed) while in archives it is not crucial to document the visual image of the artifact. Although today many archives scan their objects for accessibility, it is not a requirement.

The last point of divergence between museums, libraries, and archives is their relationship with the public. The public is accorded full range of access to the library collections in most cases, with ability to peruse a book at leisure. Not so in the museum or an archives where the irreplaceability of the work often requires viewing the object only through glass, if at all. A visitor to a library can use the cataloguing system to search for specific collections and then request to sit with them in hand. This access to full cataloguing information has not as yet become the norm in museums, although the archival world has made strides toward this end. The curator and archivist can choose to present the information that they feel is relevant.

The contents of this book highlight the similarities and differences in the digitization processes of the museum, library, and archive worlds. The many parties involved in standardizing the digitization of cultural heritage content and the proliferation of unification efforts found today underscore both the complexity and the importance of the digitization process. While the individuality of each cultural heritage institution is reflected in its customized digitization methods, the similarities between institutions should be stressed. These similarities have created a wealth of shared experiences that, if applied, will save institutions embarking on the computerization process both time and money, as they avoid mistakes. To quote Oscar Wilde, "Experience is the name everyone gives to their mistakes."[1]

Why is this book of particular importance to third millennium cataloguers? Because it will help cataloguers to digitize their collections in the most efficient way, saving time, money, and frustration. By learning from other institutions that have gone through the process, by learning from their mistakes, by being made aware of all the standards that exist, and by being given a tangible way of quantifying the project's workload and costs, the reader is better able to undertake the complexities and challenges of computerization of collections. It is the author's hope that curators, librarians, and archivists will all find this book useful, particularly when it comes to cataloguing and digitizing three-dimensional objects in a monolingual or a multilingual cultural institution.

NOTE

1. Oscar Wilde, *Lady Windemere's Fan* (Great Neck, New York: Baron's Educational Series, 1960), act III.

Acknowledgments

The author would like to thank the Israel Museum, Jerusalem (IMJ) and its administration and staff for their support in the computerization process of this highly valued national art collection. The author would especially like to thank the director of the Israel Museum, James Snyder, who has propelled the computerization project forward from the start. Within the Israel Museum's supportive environment, the author was able to experiment and reach conclusions that the author hopes will help other museums.

The author wishes to thank the members of libraries and museums, as well as the many individuals who have graciously helped with this research project. The author would particularly like to thank the database managers of the J. Paul Getty Museum, Los Angeles; the Metropolitan Museum of Art, New York; the United States Holocaust Memorial Museum, Washington, District of Columbia; the National Gallery of Art, Washington, District of Columbia; the Museum of Modern Art, New York; the Stedelijk Museum, Amsterdam; the Joods Historich Museum, Amsterdam; and Yad Vashem, Jerusalem. Learning from the people who are responsible for overseeing the computerization process, it was apparent that they bridge the two worlds of computers and arts. This role as a liaison proved to be the key to any successful project, allowing the curators and the computer programmers to share a common language. Each museum grappled with similar issues concerning computerization of its collections at different stages with varying degrees of success. Their experiences have helped the author to foresee various problems. However, these museums have not had to tackle some of the issues specific to the author's multilingual region, making the IMJ project even more of a challenge on the one hand, and more of a contribution on the other.

Without the guidance, patience, and skillful editing work of Dr. Susan Lazinger and Dr. Sheila Intner, this book would not have been completed. Copyediting was aided greatly by Joslynne Halibard. An additional acknowledgment goes to Shamira Ullman who was instrumental in introducing the *Third Millennium Cataloging Series* and its wonderful staff to the author. The author would like to express gratitude to her supportive family that has given their enthusiastic support to this book, developing their own growing interest in their rich cultural heritage.

As for possible errors and inevitable omissions, the author hopes that they will be corrected in future studies.

CHAPTER 1

The Challenges

A Review of the Literature on Computerizing Museum Collections

I n the world of museums it is the management of holdings that allows a museum to fulfill its pedagogic and preservation missions. A museum that can gear its cataloguing for the easiest and most comprehensive access will enable its curators, researchers, and the public to interact with and gain the most from these items. This book includes the theoretical aspects of museum computer systems, that is, what is available, what is used worldwide, pitfalls and successes, a case study of the computerization process, and resources at the end of each section of the book. This has been arranged with the intention of training the reader, a museum staff member, to become a collections database manager. It contains the "whos, whats, wheres, whys, and hows" of choosing and implementing the right computer system to manage museums' holdings, with specific emphasis on how to accomplish this in a multilingual setting.

BACKGROUND OF THE PROBLEM

Museums are required to register their holdings. Until now this was primarily achieved through handwritten and typed documentation. This system does not allow curators and researchers the ability to easily access required information on a daily basis. Computerization of a museum's holdings will enable the museum to accomplish this goal for the benefit of educators, students, art historians, and the general public worldwide. When holdings are registered in different languages, additional issues are raised in the process of computerizing a museum's collections, as speakers of one language may be unable to access information in the other languages.

THE CHALLENGES

Museums have found a solution to accessing the information describing their holdings by using databases. The main challenge is that most people who are trained in museum studies are not trained to implement the computerization process, while the computer programmers and implementers do not fully understand the museum world. The success of the computerization process relies on integrating art history, museology, computer science, and project management.

In addition the computerization process becomes more complicated in a multilingual environment. In this case, curators register their holdings in one of two or more languages allowing access to information via this language only, thereby excluding those who use another language.

In order to provide a nexus between the computer world and the museum world, people need to be trained to combine both fields. Museum personnel must be trained and guided through the computerization process. When two or more languages are required in a museum, the database software must be able to provide capabilities in both languages. A solution to the multilingual setting is proposed.

THE APPROACH

Our case study focuses on the Israel Museum, Jerusalem (also referred to as the IMJ or the Israel Museum in this book). The Israel Museum is in the process of moving toward a computerized database, with a particular focus on meeting multilingual needs. After studying the specific issues of the Israel Museum, and creating and implementing a process of computerization, the information was compiled to assist museum personnel in the creation of a collection's management database.

HISTORY OF THE COLLECTIONS DATABASE SYSTEMS

For the last forty years, museums worldwide have struggled to apply computer technology to the problems of collection management. These efforts have resulted in a wide variety of projects.

An early attempt at a nationwide American approach to museum computerization was made at the University of Oklahoma in 1965. A software system called GIPSY was used to automate the consolidated records of ethnographic collections held in the Oklahoma museums. This project was to serve as the pilot for an inventory of the estimated one million ethnological objects held in museums throughout the United States. Although expanded to museums in Missouri, the project never attained its goal of a national inventory and was abandoned.[1]

In the late 1960s a number of New York museums formed the Museum Computer Network (MCN) to serve as a forum for discussing the information problems common to museums. The GRIPHOS system, developed during the late 1960s and early 1970s to satisfy the specific information needs of the museum, was adopted by a number of the museums belonging to MCN group.[2]

In the early 1970s the Smithsonian Institution began devolving the SEGLEM system to replace an earlier information system, SIIR. Like GRIPHOS, SEGLEM was designed with the specific needs of museums in mind. SEGLEM was envisioned as possibly developing into a nationwide system. As SEGLEM was distributed to more and more museums, dissatisfaction arose because the implementation systems did not meet expectations. The users felt that the program was being forced upon them.

After the first wave of enthusiasm for computers subsided, museums found that they were investing a considerable amount of money in computerization with very few tangible results. As the controversy developed, individual museums began to use their own systems to meet internal needs.

Some museums used the facilities offered by the Museum Documentation Association (MDA), which was set up in 1977 to develop systems for museum documentation and act as an advisory and training agency. The MDA designed a number of computer applications and developed a formal data standard with various recording forms, cards, and registers. Thus many museums introduced computerization at a moderate cost by using the MDA system and its support structure.

During the following decades museums continued to develop their own programs without communicating with each other. Several programs could be found within each museum. Few museums could claim that they had successfully computerized their collections. There were many variations in the type of database application to the museum setting.[3]

During the 1980s there was a naiveté concerning the use of computers even among people running projects. The experience and methodologies that had been developed over the years were not shared with museums, where projects were being initiated.[4]

The situation in the United States was a reflection of the computerization process in other parts of the world during this period. In Europe other options existed, namely Adlib Museum, Sapir by IDEA and Aleph by Ex Libris. Most of the European systems are capable of multilingualism. Aleph was originally programmed for library use, but had been applied to the museum world. Although it was not well suited to the museum setting, the idea of cataloguing objects was similar, and so it was adopted in some museum institutions.

Until the mid-1980s databases had dealt only with cataloguing texts. Museums, which needed a database to support images in multiple formats, began to search for such a program. In the late 1990s, Adlib in Amsterdam and EMBARK in America (whose clients were mostly Mac users), redeveloped programs for this purpose. Gallery Systems bought EMBARK and their clients and developed a program called Museum Systems (for the PC platform). Competitors of these products include Argus (by Questor) that was also developed with museum users in mind. These products applied the multimedia capabilities of computers, which had not been addressed by the older programs.[5]

A successful museum computer system in Russia, used in many important museums, is KAMIS, developed by the "Alt-Soft" company.[6] It enables museums to create their own database as well as develop Web sites and electronic exhibition tools such as orientation stations, interactive exhibits, and information centers.

EVOLUTION OF THE HUMAN MACHINE INTERFACE IN MUSEUM DATABASE PROGRAMS

The human machine interface is the database's ability to present information to the user as well as to accept information from the user in an intuitive way.[7]

This function has been developed in the newer museum systems products. The evolution began when the early databases allowed data to enter from a client-based program. Aleph is an example of this. Following this, the ability to incorporate images and view them in the databases was added. Microsoft Access databases succeed in doing this only for small collections. The next development was to use the Internet for accessing information in the database. Argus is an example of database software with a web module. The next step occurred when museums began to upload information to the Internet. The new version of Museum Systems, which came out at the end of 2004, included this Internet option.[8]

CAN A COMMON PLATFORM BE ACHIEVED FOR THE MUSEUM WORLD?

Throughout the world each museum attempted to find solutions for its own computerization needs. Attempts have been made to bridge the different approaches by sharing information, yet this discourse can only take place when institutions share a common platform. The platforms relate to the data standards (textual and visual) and data structure (schema). The main advantage of using a unified system is that it would allow museums to share and exchange information.[9] In addition, by adhering to open standards when digitizing textual data technological obsolescence is avoided. Open standards are the most basic principles and standards that are not tied to specific software or hardware needs and are thus generic. The museum's goals should be to store their information in the most relevant (and usually complex) format for their everyday work needs. However, in order to allow this information to be interoperable the data needs to be stored in the most basic generic format. By adhering to the standards of the lowest common denominator, the data can be exported or converted to another format—or migrated.[10] The complexity of all the format choices has left a confused museum audience. The J. Paul Getty Trust & College Art Association (Getty) has filled the role of arbitrator between all the standards. (For a list of standards initiatives, see Appendix II—International and National Standards Initiatives.)

During the 1990s the Getty Institute constructed a museum lexicon of 85,000 terms for use in databases, which could support lexicon-cataloguing capabilities. This lexicon was freely distributed and thus became the integrity enforcer for many museums, creating a shared language platform by which museums could communicate. On a worldwide level this success is being duplicated. In Europe a number of institutions are translating the Getty lexicon to their local language.[11]

In order to unify the data structure used in museum databases, museums had hoped that they could achieve a unification of fields and categories similar to those found in libraries. The Dublin Core (see Appendix I—Field Names and Standards: The Dublin Core Element Set), for example, was a hard fit for the museum world, but continues to be an accepted standard. Deidre Stam writes in *Art Documentation* of the art community's efforts to devise a cataloguing code for art objects. In a detailed study of the movement,

Stam conducts a survey of the issues of automation of language with regard to describing art, specificity, varying users' needs, and the determination to somehow codify art cataloguing.[12] The J. Paul Getty Trust & College Art Association has devised it own data structure titled "Categories for the Description of Works of Art (CDWA)" (for a definition, see Murtha Baca and Patricia Harpring "List of Categories and Definitions" at http://www.getty.edu/research /conducting_research/standards/cdwa/8_printing_options/definitions.pdf).[13]

The expanded number of field names used in the Getty's CDWA element set in comparison to the compact Dublin Core element set highlights the incompatibility of fitting the book world criteria to an objects world. There are fifteen elements in the Dublin Core, but 381 fields in the CDWA! In addition to creating its own structure, the Getty has mapped its fields to other standards for data structure (see "Getty Standards Program Crosswalk of Metadata Standards" at http://www.getty.edu/research/conducting_research/standards/intrometadata/3 _crosswalks/index.html). The CDWA is mapped to other recognized schema—VRA (Visual Resources Association), MARC (Machine-Readable Cataloguing), CIMI (Computer Interchange of Museum Information), and so on. The mapping process is carried out through "crosswalks." The information can be "walked" from one data element set to another, as mapped out in comparison tables. What should be noted is that this is usually a one-way journey as described in the following scenario: The CDWA field presenting information on an artist is built up of twelve fields while in the Dublin Core there is one field. It is relatively easy for all twelve fields to be spilled or "crosswalked" from twelve to the one field but virtually impossible to reverse the process back into the twelve separate fields.[14] Despite this difficulty it is still highly recommended to map field structures to the widely used Dublin Core (see Appendix I—Field Names and Standards: The Dublin Core Element Set).

EXAMPLES OF COMPUTERIZATION PROJECTS IN MUSEUMS

Today, museums all over the world are trying to find and develop the optimal method of cataloguing and storing their collections on computers. Below is a review of four museum projects that illustrate different aspects relating to the computerization of museums: The Metropolitan Museum of Art, New York, with its use of The Museum Systems program with images; The United States Holocaust Memorial Museum, Washington, D.C., with the cataloguing, scanning, and storing of their photo archives; The Getty, Los Angeles, with its lexicon work; and Yad Vashem, Jerusalem, with its management model.

The computerization of The Metropolitan Museum of Art, New York, was prompted by a donation earmarked for image capable database software of only the textile department. A liaison with an art history background was hired from the database company to work on this project. Her role in the success of using the Gallery Systems Program was due to her ability to customize the program to meet the specific needs of the textile department. The computerization succeeded on a departmental level, yet it failed with regard to a museum-wide database. The museum's needs as an entire body were not analyzed. This resulted in a fragmented solution with a number of disparate databases working simultaneously in an uncoordinated manner. This situation was only corrected by undertaking the arduous task of comparing and mapping fields in order to combine all the data into one database.

The United States Holocaust Memorial Museum in Washington, D.C. needed four databases: Collections, Survivors' Registry, Photo Archive, and a multimedia database for the Wexler Learning Center. The museum hired a computer programmer to create databases for all but the Collections. For that, they purchased the Museum Systems (DOS version), similar to the one used at The Metropolitan Museum of Art, New York. The support company for Museum Systems was based in New York. They took too long to attend to the issues that were causing the Washington, D.C. version to halt work, and the collections database failed.[15] The other three databases of the Holocaust Museum, which were created and supported in-house, were successful.

The Getty Institute and Museum, Los Angeles, took on the project of creating a national museum lexicon. This lexicon was used in the museum in order to standardize the terminology used by the curators. This filtering system is most important in relation to information presented to the public. The Getty Museum has a team of two people in charge of filtering curatorial information and preparing it for presentation in its ArtAccess Kiosks found within the museum and partially online.[16] The team consists of an English editor, who was on the original team that created the lexicon, and a graphic editor, who deals with the images scanned. They refine the catalogued information for electronic "publishing." This system is used on one hundred objects a week. The filtering team is a necessary element in producing data worthy of public scrutiny. The lexicon project is successful on both a local and a national level.

An immense project to digitize and scan the one million "witness pages"—handwritten forms filled out from the 1950s until today, documenting people who perished during the Holocaust—was undertaken by Yad Vashem, Jerusalem, Israel.[17] They received a donation to computerize their witness pages in three months. They combined with two other companies to achieve this: Tadiran Systems (which is now owned by IBM) for the computer programming and hardware support and Manpower for human resources.

The work was divided among six hundred people who worked in two eight-hour shifts of three hundred people in three sites. Of these, thirty were administrators overseeing the project, and six were computer technicians. There were two off-campus sites, one in Jerusalem and one in Beer Sheva, and the third was on-campus. The on-campus site scanned the documents while the other two sites were responsible for typing the text they read off the digital scans. The work was overseen by the computer staff of the museum, who administered the entire project. They came to each site every day at the end of the shifts to check what issues had to be solved. These were then collected, discussed, and resolved during the night so that the workforce could continue working the next morning at 8:00 AM. The success of this undertaking was the result of Yad Vashem's efficient and organized management of a complicated project.

SUCCESSFUL DIGITIZATION PROJECTS

From the review of these collection's digitization project examples, it is evident that there are two distinct issues that need to be tackled in order to achieve a successful digitization project. One is methodical project management, and the second is the successful implementation of a mono- or multilingual database.

According to Sarasan, one of the key factors that lead to failure of museum computer projects is poor project management.[18] In *Information Technology Project Management*, Schwalbe writes that "today, new technologies have become a significant factor in many businesses. . . . These changes have fueled the need for more sophisticated projects and thus a need for more sophisticated and better project management."[19]

There is a solution. For projects to succeed they must have the following three elements: the correct type of database software should be chosen for museum work; the program chosen should be covered by support; and the computerization project should be run by someone with the knowledge of both computers and museums.

For a museum to work with a database efficiently, its database software should support cataloguing using a lexicon. Additional challenges exist in a multilingual environment, especially when considering the bidirectionality of Semitic language multilingual museums. It is recommended that in order to establish a unified vocabulary throughout the institution, a lexicon should either be purchased or created for the museum's specific needs. A lexicon often exists in the museum, if not in digital format then in paper format. It is highly recommended to build on these lists of terms in order to create a custom adapted set of unified terms. Another source of terminology is in the printed books used by the curators. For example, B. Bernstein's *Sanctification and the Art of Silversmithing* was published by the Judaica Museum of the Hebrew Home for the Aged at Riverdale in 1994 and serves many curators of Jewish museums for cataloguing Judaica. Building on the terms found in this book could serve as a foundation for a list of terms for a Jewish museum. Once applied, the list or lexicon can be used to allow cataloguing, searching, and, in multilingual situations, translating to be performed.

Implementation of a database must take into consideration that purchasing the database software is only the first stage. For a digitization project to succeed, standards need to be established and guidelines written so that the training of all museum staff members results in a unified method of cataloguing. Using a controlled vocabulary list contained in a lexicon may unify textual terminology, but not the multimedia information or the cataloguing methods. There are many other aspects of digitization that need to be addressed before the actual digitization work can take place. For example, identification of images resolution needs and field usage standards need to be given careful consideration.

RESEARCH

Museums, libraries, schools, and similar institutions have created a variety of methods to manage large quantities of information: catalogue cards, lists, and logbooks, as well as various other pen-and-paper methods, have been employed.[20] Over the last ten years, with the global move toward computerization, museums have considerably advanced toward the goal of computerizing their collections. Many have digitally catalogued both textual and visual information, and some more recently have adopted a unified museum lexicon. However, as yet, none have succeeded in achieving a fully computerized multilingual image-filled collections management database.

To find a comprehensive solution for computerization of a museum's encyclopedic holdings required examining other fields, which have implemented cataloguing, computerization, and lexicons. A methodology has been formulated by integrating information from multidisciplinary fields, such as information technology (IT), library science, and museology. The application of scientific procedures to the world of art resulted in an innovative and amalgamated approach. This combination of art and science knowledge provided a solution to the problem of computerizing multilingual museums in today's technological environment.

The IT world provided the method for database software implementation. The methods for database project management include needs analysis of end users, application and integration of the database into the work flow, testing the database, and implementation of changes for the final stage. Classification techniques and lexicons were developed from the standards found in library science. In the field of museology, in order to achieve the broadest possible understanding of the methods already employed in other museum computerization projects including those with lexicons, many projects throughout the world were studied. These included a variety of disciplines and a variety of museum environments.

METHODOLOGY

The history of computer projects in museums was reviewed, and museums worldwide were visited in order to assess their successes and failures in the computerization process. Over the course of nine years, museum site visits to more than thirty-five institutions were carried out. The site visits were supplemented with correspondence and meetings, as well as a review of Web sites and various museum databases. Work flow methods of museums were compared among a number of museums.

A questionnaire was prepared and used to assess the level of computerization in comparison with collection size and exhibition space in various museums. The museum's expectations, needs, and its relevance to future technologies were noted (see Appendix VI—Questionnaire for Museums with Answers). Following this survey of museum database use, a review of the use of databases with image capability across disciplines was done by examining literature and current Internet sites and visiting museums, libraries, auction houses, and other institutions. In order to construct a realistic budget, the time and costs involved in the project were estimated. These were based on past museum projects. These studies revealed the need for experimentation pertaining to the reuse of digital and nondigital published information found in museums. Six experiments were performed—all with the intention of learning the most efficient manner of accumulating digitized information in a generic format for conversion to the final database (see Appendix VII— Report of Experiments Recycling Data in the Museum). Concurrently to the internal studies of museum work flows, research on lexicons found worldwide was reviewed (see Appendix III—List of Currently Available Monolingual Lexicons Online). The research led to the decision that in some cases it is necessary to build a lexicon of "legacy terms" (terminology found in use in the museum both in digital format or in paper format). The defining characteristic of a lexicon, which distinguishes it from a flat table, is the network of relationships among its terms. These relationships are semantic relationships, based on logical connections among the concepts, activities, and objects represented by the terms.[21] They are often defined as a parent-child relationship ("hierarchical" term), an equivalent relationship ("alternate" term) or a related term relationship ("see also" term). Examples of these term types for the city of "Lvov" are hierarchical terms: the parent term would be Poland, and the child term would be Lvov Ghetto. Alternate terms would be Lwow or Lviv; the see also term would be Lemberg.

A number of lexicon construction projects were reviewed. These included the process used by the Israel Museum, Jerusalem, in its construction of a bilingual lexicon of eighteen thousand terms that was translated, edited, classified, and indexed in a hierarchical manner. The pilot study tested a universal formula for computerization of a percentage of holdings at a specific location while using the SAGE-K six-step process (Six-step Activation Guideline for E-Kulture). This book presents a formula derived from this research that can be utilized by museums worldwide.

THE ISRAEL MUSEUM: A CASE STUDY

Israel has approximately 180 museums, most of them in the central and northern areas. In recent years, since the founding of the State of Israel, dozens of new museums have opened. The nation's first museum is said to have been in the Greek Orthodox monastery in the Valley of the Cross, and it opened in 1865. The majority of museums in Israel are archaeological. They vary considerably in size and arrangement. Most of Israel's museums, such as those in Tel Aviv and Haifa, are public and belong either to the government or to the municipality; some, like the Israel Museum (IMJ),[22] are private.

The Israel Museum was founded in 1965 as a private, nonprofit organization operated by an independent board of trustees. It is the largest cultural institution in Israel, as well as the nation's encyclopedic museum, with four wings: Archaeology, Fine Arts, Judaica and Jewish Ethnography, and Youth. Its mission is to collect, preserve, research, and exhibit the treasures, culture, and art of the Jewish people, as well as the art, ethnography, and archaeology of the Land of Israel, and to nurture original Israeli creative arts. The Israel Museum also aspires to acquire, preserve, research, and exhibit world art from various periods and at present has a collection numbering some 270,000 objects. During an average year, the Israel Museum welcomes some 700,000 visitors.

To date, registration of these holdings had been carried out primarily through cumbersome handwritten and typed documentation, a system virtually obsolete in the twenty-first century. The computerization project was planned to advance the digital cataloguing of the Israel Museum's collections by creating a linked database to store and display images and multilingual texts, including Hebrew and English. As with many museums worldwide, the computerization process had been attempted before with varying degrees of success. This time, the goal was to look at the Israel Museum not as separate parts, that is, as departments working autonomously, but rather as one whole, unified museum.

As the Israel Museum moves toward a comprehensive system of collection management, computerization of all collection records will be essential for the optimal functioning of the encyclopedic holdings of the state's national museum. First and foremost, the Israel Museum needs to computerize its collections to facilitate the work of its staff and to assist in the effective professional interaction among its departments. Beyond providing curators, conservators, registrars, and service personnel with an efficient method for entering and updating data, computerization offers departments simultaneous access to centralized data. Curators can access conservation histories supplied by the Restoration Laboratories; the Visual Resources Department can provide visual documentation through digital imaging; the Development Department can supply credit information and exhibition histories in response to donor queries; and the Public Affairs Department can respond to collection questions quickly and accurately.

As an international museum with world-class standing, the IMJ also has an interest in and an obligation to promote scholarly and public access to the Israel Museum's collections in the broadest possible manner. Computerization of the Israel Museum's holdings will enable the museum to accomplish this goal for the benefit of curators, educators, students, art historians, and the general public worldwide.

SOLUTION TO THE PROBLEM

In order to achieve a comprehensive computerization of the Israel Museum's holdings, the author, who is the collections database manager at the IMJ responsible for the digitization project, studied other museum computerization processes and IMJ's needs. Six progressive steps were created along with a framework for lexicon integration, to guide the IMJ project from start to finish. The process was implemented as a pilot study of the complete museum database for the Israel Museum. A method was developed and modified to meet needs as they arose. The method developed is presented here for training project managers in museums worldwide and to serve as a guide for computerization projects in multilingual institutions.

NOTES

1. Rebecca A. Buck and Jean Allman Gilmore, eds., *The New Museum Registration Methods*, 4th ed. (Washington, D.C.: American Association of Museums, 1998).
2. David Vance, "The Museum Computer Network in Context," in *Museum Documentation Systems: Developments and Applications*, ed. Richard B. Light, D. Andrew Roberts, and Jennifer D. Stewart (London: Butterworths, 1986), 37–47.
3. For the application of the AthenaMuse program for the use of the MIT Museum Edgerton Collection, see Katherine Curits, "Multi-Database Support for Object-Oriented, Multimedia Authoring Environments" (PhD diss., Massachusetts Institute of Technology, Department of Civil and Environmental Engineering, May 1996).
4. Lenore Sarasan, "Why Museum Computer Projects Fail," *Museum News* 59, no. 4 (January/February 1981): 40–49.
5. For a list of collection management systems for museums, see Appendix V—A Partial List of Museum Database Programs.
6. Alt-Soft Ltd., "Information and Communication Technologies," February 28, 2003, http://www.kamis.ru/news.
7. Howard Besser, "User Interfaces for Museums" (School of Library and Information Science, University of Pittsburgh. 1989), http://www.gseis.ucla.edu /~howard/Papers/newpapers/MCN89.html#References.
8. Gallery Systems, New York, e-mail correspondence with the author, April 2002.
9. Deidre C. Stam, "The Quest for a Code, or a Brief History of the Computerized Cataloging of Art Objects," *Art Documentation* 8, no. 1 (spring 1989): 7–15.
10. The most common standards are for systems to communicate "Information and Documents—Information Retrieval" (Z39.50). For textual documents to be deliverable across a wide range of systems—XML (Extensible Markup Language), ASCII (American Standard Code for Information Interchange), and PDF (Portable Document Format) (although proprietary). Image file formats uncompressed that are platform independent include TiFF (Tagged Image File Format) and JPEG (Joint Photographic Experts Group). Moving images and studio formats include WAV and MPEG.
11. Rijksbureau voor Kunsthistorische Documentatie (RKD-Netherlands Institute for Art History), The Hague, Holland, Art & Architecture Thesaurus (AAT) translation project, http://www.rkd-db.nl/aat/index.html. The first initiative to translate the AAT in its entirety, a joint project of the Rijksbureau voor Kunsthistorische Documentatie and the Rijksdienst voor de Monumentenzorg. See Murtha Baca, "Making Sense of the Tower of Babel: A Demonstration Project in Multilingual Equivalency Work" (Los Angeles: Getty Information Institute, 1997). Other institutions are currently undertaking this translation process, for example, Centro de Documentacion de Bienes de Patrimoniales, Santiago de Chile, www.aatespanol.cl.
12. Deidre C. Stam, "The Quest for a Code, or a Brief History of the Computerized Cataloging of Art Objects," *Art Documentation* 8, no. 1 (spring 1989): 7–15.
13. In addition, the Getty Information Institute has published a standard for archives. See "Archive Standards," http://www.getty.edu/research/conducting _research/standards/introarchives/.

14. Professor Emerita Arlene Taylor of the University of Pittsburgh, "Practical Applications of Metadata" (Department of Information Science at Bar-Ilan University, Israel, workshop, April 2004).

15. United States Holocaust Memorial Museum, Washington, D.C., various museum curators interviewed by author, 1997.

16. AXS Optical Technology Resource, *ARTAccess* (Berkeley, California: AXS, 1991).

17. Interview with Michael Lieber, chief information officer, Yad Vashem, 2002. Database is accessible via http://www.yadvashem.org/lwp/workplace /IY_HON_Welcome.

18. Lenore Sarasan, "Why Museum Computer Projects Fail," *Museum News* 59, no. 4 (January/February 1981): 40–49.

19. Kathy Schwalbe, *Information Technology Project Management*, 4th ed. (Course Technology, Cambridge, Massachusetts, March 2005).

20. G. Ellis Burcaw, *Introduction to Museum Work* (Nashville, Tennessee: American Association for State and Local History, 1975).

21. See thesauri terms and relationships defined on the Getty Web site at http:// www.getty.edu/research/conducting_research/vocabularies/aat/faq.html.

22. Judith Inbar, "On the History and Nature of Museums in Israel," in *Museums and the Needs of People* (CECA Conference, Jerusalem, Israel, October 15–22, 1991).

CHAPTER 2

The Digitization Process

The SAGE-K Process of Computerizing Museum Collections

This book is intended to serve as a guide for those embarking upon a project of computerizing a museum's collection. It is intended for computer systems analysts, curators, registrars, librarians, archivists, and those who merely seek information about computerization of museum collections. The factors to be considered are the basis for computerizing museums' collections, emphasizing the specific museum at hand, databases available, managing a computerization project, analyzing the program and the museum's work flow, defining data, and running a pilot for the project. These indicate what is involved in computerizing museums' collections. Because these issues are a constant, the methodology described remains valid even though the details may change with time.

Despite the high cost of implementation, museum computerization has been and continues to be a necessary part of collections management. Changes in society, advances in technology, and the information age that we are in today have opened new avenues in museum work. At the same time museums are reaffirming their basic function—collecting, preserving, researching, exhibiting, and interpreting—but now they must expand their capabilities to include the knowledge and skills for computerization of museums' collections.

In the article entitled "Why Museum Computer Projects Fail," Sarasan writes:

> Ideally, any computer project should start with the preparation of a detailed written plan of implementation, which is developed by: analyzing the existing manual filing system; defining problems; establishing project goals; determining steps needed to achieve these goals; determining a realistic time frame for the project; determining the costs; evaluating whether the project is worth doing given projected time and costs. While these processes precede the start of most computer projects in business, few museum staff members are familiar with these steps or their importance and they are seldom followed.

DATABASE MANAGEMENT—THE PROJECT MANAGER'S GOALS

This book is the product of five years of research examining museum databases and digitization processes worldwide. The research involved interviews with the staff and an analysis of many museums, as well as visits to and an in-depth study of over thirty-five institutions, including The Metropolitan Museum of Art (The Met), The Museum of Modern Art (MOMA), The Washington National Gallery, The Getty of Los Angeles (Getty), and The Joods Historisch Museum of Amsterdam. The goal of this book is to record conclusions drawn from their experiences and to apply this knowledge in other museums.

The job of a collections database manager is to manage the museum's efforts in the installation of a museum-wide collection management database. This includes building the conceptual structure for the database, implementing this structure with the help of a local computer company, fine-tuning the database product, constructing a budget for the project, and hiring and administering a qualified team of museum staff to help implement this program. It is hoped that this guide will fill a void as there is little comprehensive written material on the subject.

The SAGE-K process outlines the essential steps in preparing to computerize a museum collection:

Step 1. Defining the museum—detailing characteristics of a museum
Step 2. Choosing database software—researching options available
Step 3. Managing the initial stages of the project, including building the budget
Step 4. Analyzing needs—streamlining the work flow in the museum so that the database reflects the work flow patterns
Step 5. Standardizing data—choosing the most suitable format of images and texts
Step 6. Running a pilot and fine-tuning the database software in reference to users' feedback

Each of the steps are discussed in greater detail in the following six chapters.

CHAPTER 3

Step 1: Defining Characteristics of the Museum

Museums come in all shapes and sizes, and not every museum needs or can afford a complicated computerization system. As a researcher would study a community in ethnographic terms, a museum can be researched using a qualitative method in order to ascertain its mechanism of functioning.[1] The first step in computerization requires understanding the characteristics of the specific museum and its needs. In regard to the computerization of museums the following questions must be raised:

- How does the museum relate to the public?
- How many curators catalogue information?
- Is there a registrar for the entire collection?

The answers to these and other questions will clarify the number of users for the database whose purpose is the cataloguing of objects. In addition, objects follow a life cycle of events. This life cycle can be monitored in a database using a module suited to tracing the activities of its catalogued objects.

MUSEUM CRITERIA

The person in charge of computerization of the museum's holdings will need to define the museum and its functions. The questionnaire included in this chapter will enable them to:

- View the entire museum comprehensively.
- Judge the physical size of the museum's grounds.
- Determine the number of objects in museum holdings.
- Establish the scope of information to be shared with the public.

A QUESTIONNAIRE

(See Appendix VI—Questionnaire for Museums with Answers, for an answer given by a museum.)

1. Name of museum.
2. Place (city, state).

3. Address.
4. Type of museum (archaeology, modern art, mixed, etc.).
5. Publicly funded/state run.
6. Size of campus (in square meters).
7. Size of museum.
8. Number of objects in collection.
9. Number of visitors per year.
10. Entrance fee (in dollars).
11. The museum is

    A. Filled with educational services/exhibition hall space only.
    B. Elitist/populist.
    C. Family oriented/group oriented/single-visitor oriented.

12. Popular times for museum visits—free time/weekends/vacations.
13. Average length of stay in the museum—twenty minutes/two hours/four hours.
14. Most popular exhibit at this time and why.
15. If you could prepare an exhibit, what subject matter would interest you most?
16. The museum has guided tours—often /infrequently /not at all.

    A. Are the guides students or retirees?
    B. Are they paid or volunteer staff?
    C. Does the museum offer audio guides (handheld devices)?

17. Does the museum make use of computers?

    A. Is there a database for the curator's everyday work needs?
    B. Are there kiosks for the public containing multimedia, virtual exhibits, the Internet?
    C. Is there a searchable database of the museum's collection?
    D. Are there other computerization projects in or outside the museum campus?
    E. Is there external access to the collection via an Internet site?
    F. What is the URL address?
    G. Does the Internet site give information pertaining to the holdings in the collection (i.e., via a searchable database)?

18. Does the museum sell image rights to the public?

    A. How much does it cost for a visitor to purchase the rights to use an image, for example, for publication in a doctoral book?
    B. Can the image be sent as a digital file?
    C. What resolution (dpi and size of image in megabytes) and which format (JPEG, tiff)?

19. Is there a gift shop at the museum?
20. Are there food areas in the museum?
21. How many publications a year does the museum produce? Are these exclusively sold in the gift shop?

RESULTS OF QUESTIONNAIRE

The answers to the questionnaire will supply a comprehensive overview of the museum's characteristics. Focusing on questions 6, 7, 8, and 9 will establish the museum's size and determine the modules required for application of the database software to the collection. Question 17 assesses the present computerization level in the museum.

GRADING SYSTEM FOR MUSEUM'S SIZE

After analyzing the answers provided by museums to the questionnaire (see Appendix VI—Questionnaire for Museums with Answers, for an answer given by a museum), it is possible to conclude the following. Museums can be classified according to two criteria: (1) size (Table 3.1) graded small, medium, and large, and (2) museum computer usage (Table 3.2) graded 0 through 4.

By using these grades the Israel Museum, our case study, can be categorized as "Large/#4." This is because it has over 270,000 objects and does not have a full database for all curators but does have a few databases for four of its fifty curators. These criteria help us to understand the needs of a museum in relation to its database and function. In essence, if a single registrar and a curator run a museum[2] a smaller database is necessary, and it would be inappropriate to apply the same system used by a large museum with tens of curators and departments. All museums can benefit from a database for organizing and digitizing their collections, but budgets and standards differ in large and small museums. In this book, however, we focus on the needs of medium and large museums and not the needs of small museums.[3]

In most museums reviewed, it had been decided that all staff members who add data or information about the state and status of an object would have access to the database while a few stations would be used for administrative purposes. In addition to using an Internet browser (i.e., Microsoft Internet Explorer, Mozilla Firefox, Netscape, etc.) on other museum computing stations, additional museum staff could have access to search the collections database via the Intranet. Intranet can only be viewed by computer stations within the museum departments. Internet resides in the public domain and can be viewed freely by all.

TABLE 3.1 Museum size

	Size Sq. Meters	No. Objects	No. Visitors/ Year
Small	<300	<1000	<3,000
Medium	300 > 3000	1000 > 100,000	3,000 > 250,000
Large	>3000	>100,000	>250,000

TABLE 3.2 Museum computer usage

Museum Computer Usage Graded	
#0	None or Windows/Word
#1	Curators with database system
#2	Public access to database from within museum
#3	Public access to database outside of museum
#4	Public use of data output (i.e., images, texts) via Internet site

TABLE 3.3 Example of questionnaire results in regard to database software options

Size of Museum	Grade Applied to Recommended Database Software Options		
	Grade 0–2 Recommended: Flat Table	Grade 3 Recommended: Rational Table	Grade 4 Recommended: Database with Internet Images and Basic Multilingual Capabilities
Small (1–5 users)	Off the shelf table, e.g., Excel	Off the shelf, general database, e.g., Microsoft Access	Off the shelf, cataloguing museum system, e.g., The Museum System Light
	Avg. cost: $2,000	Avg. cost: $5,000	Avg. cost: $100,000 plus per-user and server costs
Medium (6–20 users)	Off the shelf table, e.g., Excel	Off the shelf, general database, e.g., Microsoft Access	Off the shelf, customizable cataloguing museum system, e.g., Museum System or Argus
	Avg. cost: $2,000	Avg. cost: $5,000	Avg. cost: $250,000 plus per-user and server costs
Large (21–100 users)	Off the shelf, simple database, e.g., Microsoft Access	Off the shelf, complex relational database, e.g., Sapir Enterprise	Off the shelf, customizable cataloguing museum system with web export capabilities, e.g., Museum System or Argus with all modules
	Avg. cost: $5,000	Avg. cost: $35,000	Avg. cost: $400,000 plus per-user and server costs

APPLYING RESULTS TO DATABASE SOFTWARE OPTIONS

The results of the questionnaire helped define criteria by which one can "grade" museums (see Table 3.3). This grade can then be applied to choosing the appropriate database software for the museum.[4]

The particulars of how to make these decisions, choosing the right database software and tools, are discussed in chapter 4 (Step 2). For a small museum, the cost of the grade 3 and 4 computerization can be prohibitive and the expansiveness of the programs excessive.

NOTES

1. David M. Fetterman, *Ethnography: Step by Step*, 2nd ed. (Thousand Oaks, California: Sage, 1998).
2. Mary Case, ed., "Registrars on Record: Essays on Museum Collections Management" (Washington, D.C.: Registrars Committee of the American Association of Museums, 1988).

3. Neal Arminta, *Exhibits for the Small Museum—A Handbook* (Nashville, Tennessee: American Association for State and Local History, 1976). Reflects on a partial definition for small museums.

4. For a list of computer databases for museums, see Appendix V—A Partial List of Museum Database Programs. All prices listed are approximated and refer to the purchase of the database program with licenses for users. No other costs are included here (server storage disk space or backup tapes, ISP Services, hosting, IT, etc.).

CHAPTER 4

Step 2: Choosing a Database System

According to *Merriam-Webster's Collegiate Dictionary* a database is defined as "a usually large collection of data organized especially for rapid search and retrieval (as by a computer)."

Museum staff has many daily tasks to perform. These include corresponding with donors, counting inventory, preparing for exhibitions, and selling rights to image use. A database system enables easy access to a myriad of information connected to an object and is needed for the following tasks: the basic information (its origin, year, artist, etc.), supplementary information (donor names and addresses, etc.), and history (background, cost, labels, insurance, exhibitions, etc.).

APPLICATIONS FOR THE DATABASE SYSTEM IN A MUSEUM

Databases and the information they contain play a major role in issues pertaining to international repatriation and "lost art." "Lost art" can be understood from the following examples. One of the great unmentionables of museum practices has been the *sub rosa* acquisition of objects with less-than-favorable provenance.[1] Recently the acquisition of objects by museums during the Second World War and later has been a well-publicized legal issue. A database of "lost art" of the Holocaust has been requested by families who have come to major museums in search of their inheritance. An example in which the database played an important role was in the British courts' ruling in London that museums are required to give public access to objects acquired by the museums during the relevant periods. A museum in London gave access to its entire collection via the web to solve its judicial problems, whereas other museums allowed public scrutiny of objects acquired only over the period of time in question. Without having a searchable database, this project would have been cumbersome if not impossible.[2]

Researchers turn to museums every day for help in obtaining information on religious and ethnic subjects as varied as prayer, jewelry, or costumes from specific periods. In short, the database is a useful tool both for public access and as an aid for the curator in his/her daily work.

DATABASE SYSTEMS: CUSTOM OR OFF-THE-SHELF

Museums are wary about purchasing database systems for a number of reasons. In particular, museums balk at purchasing costly database systems, fearing that today's choice may not be the latest and/or the best because of the rapidly changing technology. The question often raised in museums is, "Will today's choice stop us from having the latest and best tomorrow?" A museum must find one format that solves most of its needs and then remain loyal to it, adapting it as necessary. Over time there may appear newer or better products, but if the chosen database software is adequate, there should be no reason to change to another system.[3]

There are two approaches to purchasing database systems for computerizing collections. The first approach uses a custom-built database system and the second an off-the-shelf product. Philip Greenspun of Massachusetts Institute of Technology (MIT) offers a creative recommendation: use databases constructed from free software found on his or other sites. The database would be viewed using a free web browser (that comes standard in computers, such as Internet Explorer or Netscape) by way of a museum-wide Intranet.[4] The advantages of a custom-built product are that the initial costs are cheaper than an off-the-shelf product, and because it is custom built the needs of the museum are met exactly. The disadvantage of a truly customized product is that the museum is the first to use the program and must work through the first stage problems and "bugs." The correction of these bugs and development costs in the long-term prove to be expensive. Being a maiden system, it does not derive benefit from previous or future users. An off-the-shelf product continues to be updated following the development needs of all its users. In most cases these updates are passed along to all the program users in the next version updates.

Most museums choose to buy an off-the-shelf product even though at the outset it is more expensive. In the long term it will turn out to be cheaper because it is a tried-and-true solution. Tony Gill, in the *Guide to Computers in the Museum Documentation Association* (MDA) publication of 1996, reviews the advantages and disadvantages of the "do it yourself" database. He says while at first it may seem inexpensive and the user has maximum control "a certain amount of skill and considerable amount of time will be needed in order to produce a robust and useful application and support will only be available from the individuals who wrote the application if at all. The disadvantage of dependence on individual employees is often encapsulated (somewhat morbidly) by the 'under a bus' scenario."[5]

As museums implement these off-the-shelf products, the providers refine and improve the programs based on the museum needs, so that buying a product like this brings with it the accumulated experience of many museums and therefore has advantages. Despite the benefits, when programs cross linguistic borders or are needed in multilingual settings, they require complicated and costly customization. In addition, Semitic languages poses a complication as they read from right to left, and thus all the numbers (dates and accession codes, etc.) are flipped, as is punctuation.[6]

The inflexibility of an off-the-shelf product is a major disadvantage. Local support and, more important, in-house support are absolutely necessary if a product is to succeed. As the product is off-the-shelf, it is meant to be a "one-size-fits-all" solution, in essence not fitting anyone.

The strength of the off-the-shelf product lies in the fact that many museums already use this product. Their usage and feedback have created a product that can satisfy many needs.

DATABASE SOFTWARE ACCESSORIES

Databases are not able to supply solutions to all curatorial cataloguing needs. For this reason accessories are supplied (at additional cost). These accessories are often referred to as modules, as they are modular and can be added later. They may include options for using a bar code scanner which could speed cataloguing; an option for cataloguing images outside the database, which helps to manage multiple resolution of images (thumbnail, midsize, or archival); an Internet module which enables the information to be accessed via a Web site. The report and screen interfacing options may also be included as modules.

REPORTS AND SCREEN INTERFACING OPTIONS

The usefulness of database software interfacing[7] in relation to the image is a priority for curators. The Graphic User Interface (GUI)[8] of the screens that present the thumbnails must reflect the image's purpose. The way of handling the image, that is, moving, drag and drop to categorize, and double click to open is also important. In addition to the image factors, the order in which the fields are presented on the screen must be decided. Some databases allow the fields and images to be reorganized to suit the user. Reports give an added dimension of flexibility to the presentation of data. It is best if reports can be saved as a Word document (not always an option). Crystal Reports is an example of a program that can be added to most databases for printing and saving reports with the option of saving the reports as a Word file. Business Objects has the option of saving in RTF, Excel, or HTML formats—the latter can include images.

THE INTERNET

Museums have a new window for the public to access their information—the museum Web site.[9] This is the perfect place to allow partial access to database information. For this purpose a web browser could be used to view the data.[10] Many databases include an option to upload "on the fly" (in real-time) to the Internet. This will allow the interfacing options to employ the web browser, with its multiplatform capabilities, as a data entry tool.

THE STORAGE SERVER AND SUPPORT TEAM

Both options, the off-the-shelf or the custom-made database systems, require that the museum consider that any database software package needs two additional elements for an operative system: the server with a database administrator (DBA) and the database support staff, specifically a local company for support and a full-time in-house database manager

There are a number of servers to choose from, including IBM's DB2, Oracle, or Microsoft SQL Server. In Greenspun's online books, his aim is to convince the public that in most cases Oracle can be replaced by MYSQL.[11] This would prevent the high cost and the "particular appetite for feeding and caring" of Oracle by a DBA.[12] In analogous terms, a server, used for storage, is like a refrigerator. Oracle can be compared with a refrigerator inside an automobile. Most people just need the refrigerator, and can save on the future repairs that come with more machinery.[13] Nonetheless, many museums have chosen Oracle. This decision can be influenced by many factors. For example, in Israel, Oracle has addressed the Hebrew language problems and provides good local support, and therefore at present Oracle is a good choice for a museum in Israel. The Getty, among other museums, works with Oracle because they decided that the benefits justify the cost.

There are two other important players in the support system. One is the local support company. Its role includes a thorough needs analysis, product customization, and, if necessary, translation for localization of interfacing. Once the database software is up and running, it will attend to most day-to-day issues and complicated problems as they arise. The size of the company may be a factor to consider: The longevity of a small company remains questionable; a large company may be around longer but not have the time to focus on the specific requirements of the museum. This should be considered when purchasing a program and finding support for it. The other important support player is the database manager within the museum, who serves as the liaison between the support company and the museum.

Customization of the product (e.g., which fields are needed, which language is more important, etc.) varies with the needs of each user and requires an in-house person to customize each user's product, as the off-the-shelf product leaves little room for the amateur to maneuver.

CHOOSING AN OFF-THE-SHELF DATABASE SYSTEM

Once the museum decides that its collections can benefit from a database system and has the staff and/or external support in place to host, store, and maintain a database server, the museum is ready to purchase a database software product. Research by the author shows that for medium and large museums, to buy an off-the-shelf product is more economical than building one from scratch; the many complications that arise when using a custom-built database system in these museums add dramatically to the final cost of the program. Small museums, on the other hand, can work well with homemade tables to support their work and can later upgrade to the more complete (and complicated) off-the-shelf programs as needed. Therefore this book focuses on the needs of medium- and large-size museums. In medium- and large-size museums it is recommended to purchase an off-the-shelf program (for a list of program options, see Appendix V—A Partial List of Museum Database Programs) and fine-tune the database system, so that it can best fit each individual museum's needs. In order to review the possible choices, it is necessary to research the currently available database software products, investigating the possibility of local support and service for the ones that fill the museum's needs. Choosing the correct computer program is a long and arduous task. There are many variables to consider. A three-phase process that can be used to investigate the capabilities of the collections management programs reviewed, testing these abilities, and judging the test results of the programs is included in this chapter. Building a comparison table listing these test results is beneficial (see "Phase Three" for a table comparing database software test results of two collection management programs). The entire museum staff should be involved in this decision to ensure satisfaction and cooperation when the final database software is chosen and implemented.

For the museum's needs, the success of the database software depends on the following attributes: local support, multilingual capabilities (Western and Semitic languages including diacritics, Cyrillic, and other alphabets), and flexibility of the product's fields. The quality and stability of the support company are critical.

THE GLOBALIZATION OF A DATABASE SYSTEM—ITS CHALLENGES

Most database systems are constructed with the culture of the hosting country in mind. Today there are many companies producing database systems that are interested in globalization, that is, applying their database systems to other cultures and languages. This can be attributed to the spread of ethnic pride, which brought to the forefront the need for multilingual database capabilities. This counteracts the idea, which was popular during the last decade, that the world would adopt one language for all computer programs (specifically English, as on the Internet). A single language in a database (foreign or local) would appear as a single column of information within the tables of the database.

In some cases the globalization took the form of the database as being bilingual. For example, American museums are requesting databases that can support Spanish and English, Canadian museums need French and English, and Israeli museums require Hebrew and English.

Bilingual databases need to accept information into two parallel columns, which relate one to the other. One of the first problems that arise in this situation is that the ASCII code of 128 characters cannot simultaneously put forth a letter in two or more alphabets. Frequently letters overlap, for example, pressing "e" accent produces the third Hebrew letter. This problem led to the standardization of Unicode, which can accommodate a large number of languages simultaneously. This remapping of all the universal characters so that no letter sits on the space of another should allow true globalization of the database, with two or more parallel columns of information found in the multilingual databases.

THE GOALS AND RESPONSIBILITIES OF THE SUPPORT COMPANY FOR THE DATABASE

The database software must be chosen only after a support company is found locally which will be able to provide maintenance. The importance of this fact cannot be sufficiently stressed. It is useless to buy an expensive piece of machinery (like a car) if there is no one to service it (as anyone with an imported car and no parts in the local garage can verify).

The support company works hand-in-hand with the database manager. The database manager acts as a liaison with the museum, while the database company confirms the requests it is able to fulfill and determines whatever is not within the framework of the chosen database system.

The fine-tuning and customization of the database software is attended to by the support company, which has an interest in the success of the database within the walls of the museum. The knowledge of the database system and its attributes will be essential when analyzing the application of the database system to the museum's work needs in the needs analysis.

The process of choosing the museum's database software consists of three phases:

> Phase 1—Writing a request for proposal (RFP) that defines the criteria of the database software in general terms
> Phase 2—Sending a standard test package to the applicants who matched the criteria
> Phase 3—Judging the abilities of the applicants based on results of the test administered in the package

PHASE 1—RFP: CRITERIA FOR DATABASE SOFTWARE FOR BILINGUAL MEDIUM AND LARGE MUSEUMS

An RFP is an invitation for suppliers to bid on a specific product or service. Sometimes an RFP is preceded by a request for information (RFI). This is used to determine what products and services are potentially available in the marketplace to meet a customer's needs. RFIs are commonly used on major procurements, where a requirement could potentially be met through several alternate means. An RFI, however, is not an invitation to bid, is not binding on either the buyer or sellers, and may or may not lead to an RFP.[14]

An RFP typically involves more than the price. Other requested information may include basic corporate information and history, financial information, technical capability, product information such as stock availability and estimated completion period, and customer references that can be checked to determine a company's suitability.

RFPs often include specifications of the collections management program. The more detailed the specifications, the better the chances that the proposal provided will be accurate. Generally RFP's are sent to an approved vendor list or are publicly advertised.

Appropriate applicant companies are those that fulfill the criteria outlined in the RFP. The applicant companies return a proposal by a set date and time. The proposals are used to evaluate the suitability of the database company.

Discussions may be held with the applicants on the proposals (often to clarify technical capabilities or to note errors in a proposal). All or only selected bidders may be invited to participate in a subsequent test of applicants.

An RFP containing the minimum requirements and specifications for a system to manage collections is usually drawn up by a database expert after analyzing the museum's needs.

CHARACTERISTICS OF A REQUESTED BILINGUAL DATABASE SYSTEM

For multilingual institutions the suggested system should support both a primary and a secondary language simultaneously, allowing for entry of object cards in either language, and for instructions to be given and search engines to operate in both languages.

For all the collections, there are universal common fields, as well as some unique fields. The committee should see if the system is flexible enough to add fields, rename them, and change the order in which they are listed.

The system should be able to display all types of images, manipulate them, and view them close up.

The system should be built in a manner that will allow for different levels of access, for example, curator/registrar/general public. It should be possible to assign and change authorization as needed, as well as to define certain fields as hidden.

Only the curator should be able to have access to the full range of images and texts (around eighty fields). The tasks that the curators have to do on a day-to-day basis, such as tracking the movement of objects to and from the conservation and photo labs, should be simple. The registrar should have access to the information needed to register objects (around twenty-four fields). The public should be able to access the objects via the Internet with the use of a search engine. They will be able to see a limited amount of information (around twelve fields), including images and sounds.

It might be necessary for the system to process and to convert information into a bilingual lexicon that will include tens of thousands of terms and names in a hierarchical manner.

The search mechanism needs to be accessible, easy to use, and, in some cases, bilingual. It should be possible to search within the database system, including partial words, and to search within lexicon fields and free-text fields. Searches within lexicon fields in one language should give results that would include results for the same term in the second language. After receiving the results of the search, it should be possible to search additional terms that are found in the results from the first search, for example, to search for objects from the same artist.

The system must be able to generate reports with cross-sections and by requirements. The reports will include images and bilingual capabilities. The system should also be capable of easily saving reports and creating and saving templates in a flexible and convenient manner.

A full Internet module, which will include searches, entry into particulars of an object, and viewing of images must be provided.

A local company will be needed to provide support for the system at any given time.

PHASE 2—TESTING THE APPLICANTS

Following the receipt of responses from appropriate applicant companies that fulfill the criteria outlined in the RFP, a test should be administered in order to see the database systems in a more in-depth way. The applicant companies are invited to present their proposed solution to the test before a panel of judges. The panel should include representatives from the legal, administrative, technological, and professional staff of the museum.

The test, administered by the museum, should provide the database companies with material from its collections, including textual descriptions, terminology from the lexicon, and images. These actual examples will help the museums to judge the results better, as it is more relevant to review museum data in the database program than hypothetical material.

Below is an example of a test with an appendix containing data that could be employed in the database company's presentation.[15] A hypothetical bilingual museum has been chosen as an example. The hypothetical museum contains three types of collections: fine arts, archaeology, and ethnology. A test is given for each collection.

THE TEST—FINE ARTS

Search for all works by Prins by entering the name "Prins" in the "artist" field (see Table 4.1).

Search results should include all works by the artist Prins, catalogued in either the primary or secondary language, and thumbnail images with captions (see Figure 4.1).

When the image is pressed, a large image will pop-up with all relevant textual data.

The results should include access to lexicon and data on Prins (including basic facts such as when he lived, country of birth, where he worked).

THE TEST—ARCHAEOLOGY

After inserting data from Figure 4.2, search for objects using two fields simultaneously: the lexicon field object name = "lamp" and in the descriptive free text field = "color-coated ware."

Search results should include all objects where the object name scroll (including conjugations, e.g., scrolls, scrolled) and the words "color-coated ware" exist in the descriptive free-text and thumbnail images with captions.

When the image is pressed, a large image will pop-up with all relevant textual data.

It should be possible to receive additional information linking to other objects relating to any one particular field of interest within the search results, for example, to cross-reference all objects of the same time period.

THE TEST—ETHNOLOGY

Look in the lexicon field country = "Near East" including variations, then search for all objects where country = "Near East."

Search results should include all objects where country = "Near East."

Information should be available to the users according to their access-rights. See the following example of access to data according to authorizations using visual and textual information from Figure 4.3:

1. The curator has access to all images. Clicking on the thumbnail will bring up a full-sized image and all the relevant data. The curator can add and update data. It will be possible to examine the images closely with Zoom (magnifying glass). There will be an option to open a video clip or map of the Near East.
2. The registrar can click on the thumbnail and view the full-sized image and relevant data, but not make any changes.
3. The public at large can see only the thumbnails with whatever information is contained in the label.
4. All users can link to other objects relating to their particular field of interest.

APPENDIX TO THE TEST

The appendix to the test is made up of data to be entered into the database reviewed. The data supplied for the test includes Figures 4.1, 4.2, 4.3, and Table 4.1.

FIGURE 4.1   Fine arts image example from appendix to the test

Benjamin Prins (1860–1934, Amsterdam, Holland)
Fruitmeisje (Fruitseller), c.1916
Oil on canvas
36 × 50cm
Private Collection, Jerusalem

Photo © with permission from a Private Collection, Jerusalem, 2006.

FIGURE 4.2   Archaeology image example from appendix to the test

Roman oil lamp

Dorchester, Dorset
Mid-First Century
Wessex Archaeology Collection

Dorchester has preserved many archaeological finds from its Roman past when it was called Durnovaria. Before building work began on the hospital site, Wessex Archaeology was asked to excavate for possible remains. The excavation, carried out in 2000 and 2001, was the largest archaeological investigation of the town for many years.

One major discovery by Wessex Archaeology was a Roman mosaic dating to about 350 AD at the former County Hospital site in Dorchester in Dorset. Excavation on the eastern side of the site revealed that wooden buildings had been put up in the mid-first century. Slots for timber beam-foundations and rubbish pits were found, as well as two stone-built ovens. Soil removed from the ovens was found to be full of herringbones so they may have been used for making a strong fish sauce called garum, an essential part of Roman cooking.

This little oil lamp, found at this site as well, is made from color-coated ware (the hardened clay is dipped in colored slip before firing). It comes from the earlier building on the site, one of the houses bordering the western side of the street. The handle by which it was once carried is now broken, as are the small lugs on either side which held cords to suspend it when lit. The face decoration above the oil chamber is just visible.

Photo © with permission of Wessex Archaeology.

TABLE 4.1   Lexicon example from appendix to the test

Primary English	Secondary Hebrew	Dates	Birthplace	Birthplace Hebrew	Editing Source	Role English	Role Hebrew
Prins, Benjamin	בנימין פרינס,	1860–1934	Holland	הולנד	RKD	Painter | sculptor	פסל|אמן

FIGURE 4.3   Ethnology image example from appendix to the test

Hebrew Inscribed Amulet
Near East, Nineteenth Century
Case: Silver
Scroll: Parchment
L: 12 cm
Private Collection, Jerusalem

Photo © with permission from a Private Collection, Jerusalem, 2006.

PHASE 3—COMPARING RESULTS OF TWO COMPANIES

After the presentations, each company's solution to the test should be graded on a scale of 0 to 5, with 5 as the highest score. See Table 4.2 which illustrates how two companies might be evaluated after completing the phases 1 and 2 described above. Table 4.2 grades the test results for each section of the test and summarizes both in a total numerical grade and in a textual summarization of the qualities of each company's products. This quantification is helpful in deciding which product to purchase for a computerization project.

TABLE 4.2 Comparing score results of two database companies

	Company 1	Grade	Company 2	Grade
Language	Bilingual	5	English product with a promise to translate.	4
Fields	Has many fields missing and would need to develop them.	2	Has the flexibility the museum needs.	5
Interfacing (how the screen looks)	Has all the necessary elements, while allowing access to the "guts" so that field and list changes can be made. However, it lacks the "finish" and is therefore less visually attractive than Company 2.	4	Has experience in museum work, apparent in its breadth and range. Interfacing has flexible tabs and fields.	5
Customization	Willing to sit with us (locally) and make these changes (initially and later).	5	Standardized so "you get what you see." Critical changes will be done in the United States by the company and added to its next updated program.	3
Input of Information	Has a program called "soundex" which is meant to catch like-words and prevent the system from duplicate spelling (it is not infallible). Makes use of drop-down boxes which are very easy to update, which help in search efficiency, once again preventing free text errors. More user friendly, with its bilingual drop-down boxes.	5	Has not yet been translated, and so it is too early to say if they are capable of mimicking the product that Company 1 has produced which can have terms in both languages viewed simultaneously. Company 2 has a lexicon, which complicates input but helps in output (searches). Possibly their lexicon can solve most problems associated with its translation.	4

	Company 1		Company 2	
OUTPUT OF INFORMATION	Limited number of reports, but simple output of reports. Search capabilities within a field as in free text.	4	1. Company 2 purchased a group of templates that aid in printing reports (in English). Company 1 could also do this. The program also has the ability to build custom reports. 2. Field searches possible. No free text searches.	4
Company Experience	Company 1 is a small company with little museum experience. Daughter company of Company 1 with a questionable future.	2	Company 2 has experience translating programs and has a large company with a good name. Company 2's weak spot in the past has been in its product support.	5
Support	Local support through Company 1's skeleton company. The museum will need to establish an in-house support department.	3	Local support through a daughter company. The museum will need to establish an in-house support department.	5
Costs: Present and Future	$80,000 = paying for potential.	4	$225,000 + customization costs = paying for experience.	5
Conclusion	An incomplete product. Flexible. Local support. Translated. Needs programming work.	34	A complete product. Flexible. Local support. Not translated, but has done such work in the past.	40

NOTES

1. John W. Hoopes, "The Future of the Past: Archaeology and Anthropology on the World Wide Web" (Department of Anthropology and Museum of Anthropology, the University of Kansas, paper prepared for the symposium *The Potential of Museum Web Sites for Research* at Museums on the Web: An International Conference, Los Angeles, California, March 16–19, 1997), http://www.ku.edu/~hoopes/mw/. (Sponsored by the Getty Information Institute and organized by Archives & Museum Informatics.)
2. For a sample list of Web sites listing art stolen during the Holocaust, see http://www.lostart.de/links/index.php3?lang=english.
3. The shelf life of a database is often noted as between seven and ten years. What this means is that the data needs to be migrated to a new database at that time. It does not mean (hopefully) that the information needs to be rekeyed! By following standards when setting up the database, the migration process is more successful. For more on this subject, see the section beginning with Obsolescence in chapter 7.
4. Philip Greenspun, Computer Science and Artificial Intelligence Laboratory, Massachusetts Institute of Technology, personal e-mail, November 25, 1998. In this letter Greenspun refers to his online book at http://philip.greenspun.com/panda/. More recently a hardcover book was published by Eve Andersson, Philip Greenspun, and Andrew Grumet, *Software Engineering for Internet Applications* (Cambridge, Massachusetts: MIT Press, 2006), http://philip.greenspun.com/seia/?.
5. Tony Gill, *MDA Guide to Computers in Museums*, chapter 3 (Cambridge, UK: Museum Documentation Association, 1996). He concludes with a tip: "Ensure any do-it-yourself database projects are comprehensively documented."
6. In 1998 the author was a beta tester for PhotoShop Middle East. KARAT, an Israeli Support Company for Adobe, began Hebraizing the successful PhotoShop program. The author can conclude from this experience that the product, which was expected to be done in nine months, took more than a year and a half to complete, and leaves a lot to be desired.
7. Interfacing—Front-end, user end of the screen.
8. Graphic User Interface (GUI)—The users' instinctive use of the tools is a science based on the anatomical morphology combined with human motion.
9. The topic of museum Web sites is not within the scope of this book. There are many good sources of information and a multitude of museum Web sites from which one can learn. For some examples of museum Web sites worldwide, see Georgina Buckley, *Australian Visual Arts Internet Resources* (Canberra, ACT: Australian National University Library, 1999), http://anulib.anu.edu.au/clusters/ita/subjects/austvisres.html. A good source for the theories behind museum Web sites is John W. Hoopes, "The Future of the Past: Archaeology and Anthropology on the World Wide Web," *Archives & Museum Informatics* 11, no. 2 (1997): 87–105, http://www.ku.edu/~hoopes/mw/.
10. Jim Agnus reviews some techniques in his site titled "Managing Your Museum Web Site," Ed-Resources.Net, http://www.ed-resources.net/mw99/. On this site, Agnus reviews tools and techniques that will allow museums to provide twenty-four-hour-a-day access to extensive stores of cultural information and to provide that information in an attractive package. Discussion headings:

Planning, Design Standards and Guidelines, Devising Content, Measuring Success and Marketing.

11. Philip Greenspun, http://philip.greenspun.com/panda/.
12. Philip Greenspun, personal e-mail, 1998, see note 4.
13. David Guedalia, chief technology officer of Mobilee, interview with author, January 1999, phone conversation, Beit Shemesh, Israel.
14. Wikipedia Web site, "Request for Proposal," http://en.wikipedia.org/wiki /Request_For_Proposal.
15. The Canadian Heritage Information Network (CHIN) published a different test on their Web site. See "Collections Management Software Review— Criteria Checklist," http://www.chin.gc.ca/English/Collections_Management /Software_Selection/English/Doc/criteria_checklist.doc.

CHAPTER 5

Step 3: Prelude to the Computerization Project

SOCIALIZING THE IDEA WITHIN THE MUSEUM

Once the project is approved by the museum administration, work is necessary to create a cooperative environment among museum staff. The guidelines and principles that help shape the thought process in the creation of the database must be shared with the curators and the end users. To achieve this, the project manager, in association with the museum registrar and the Museum Computers and Systems Department head, should form a team to run the project and work with the general museum staff to ensure its success.

The first step in socializing the database project among the greater museum staff is to create two steering committees for reporting and feedback purposes. The first committee, the Curatorial Steering Committee, is made up of representatives of different museum departments who are administrative staff with direct authority over departmental personnel and museum content. The decisions reached in these meetings will guide the project and affect museum subdepartmental staff work. The second steering committee, or Executive Committee, sits in parallel to the Curatorial Steering Committee, and is in charge of overseeing costs. It is made up of the museum directors, head of finances, head of fundraising, and a chairperson from the Curatorial Steering Committee who represents that group's needs. The decisions reached at these meetings represent the convergence of the curatorial needs with the reality of the funding abilities of the museum. Both committees should meet on a biannual basis.

BUDGETING FOR THE PROJECT

There are two types of staff necessary for the project: the database support staff, which manages the actual database program and trains the users, and the data entry staff, which inputs data into the program. As personnel is the most expensive part of the project budget, it is important to decide what existing staff are prepared to work on the project and if additional skills are necessary.

The database support staff are the people who work directly with the database from the computer end. They consist of the program manager, program integrator, coordinator of digital texts, and coordinator of digital graphics.

The program manager works as the liaison between the museum staff and the computer programmers. This person should coordinate the disparate groups that contribute to the entire database project. The manager is responsible for bringing everyone together to create a successful project.

The role of liaison is an important key to a successful project. The manager acts as a bridge between the two worlds of computers and arts, enabling the curators and the computer programmers to share a common language. The support company works hand-in-hand with the program manager. The manager helps the museum to express its needs, while the database company confirms the requests it is able to fulfill and decides what is not within the framework of the chosen program.

Acting as a liaison with the curatorial staff of the departments in the museum, the program manager works to define user requirements in order to develop a museum-wide information system. The manager oversees the work of the staff and the implementation of the program into the museum's work flow process.

The task of converting older databases into the current program falls within the program manager's realm.

Working with the Internet Department and the Visual Rights and Reproductions Department, the program manager also aids in the proliferation and distribution of the assets found in the museum database to the curators, researchers, and the public via kiosks on the museum campus and via the Internet.

When using a database program that allows for customization of reports and field names, the program integrator is the person who customizes them according to user needs. An ability to work with the museum staff, understand their needs, and apply their requests to create a more user-friendly program is most important.

Museums have many types of users, each one with different access rights. The program integrator adjusts the program to the clients individually so that they can access the information they need for their daily tasks. Using the database reports system or other external report software, the program integrator creates reports that answer the users' needs.

As there are many different users, it is essential to ensure that data is entered into one format. The coordinator of digital texts must be skilled in data entry in various formats, using different programs. Also, in order to create unity, the coordinator needs to map fields from different databases found in the museum. Therefore, this person must understand the individual work methods of the museum staff members.

The coordinator of digital texts will be required to teach data entry skills to the various museum members who will be using the database in their departments and be on hand to give help where needed. If outsourced staff is used, then they too need to be trained according to the museum's standards for data digitization.

The legacy terms from the lexicon need to be indexed, and, as curators create new terms, their integrity must be managed. The coordinator of digital texts must have the ability to translate and edit texts for use within the database and to ensure the integrity and quality of all data entered in the museum.

The coordinator of digital graphics is responsible for assigning access rights for each user on the server. This coordinator also verifies that there is enough storage space on the server to continue scanning, and standardizes scanning and saving procedures. The coordinator of digital graphics ensures that the same procedures are followed for all new scans and that they are saved on the server in a uniform manner.

The coordinator of digital graphics works with the museum staff to show them how to scan pictures, negatives, and slides; in what format to save them; what they should be called; and where to store them. If outsourced staff is used then they too need to be trained according to the museum's standards for image digitization. The coordinator oversees all follow-up graphic work necessary to conform to the institution's standards for digital images, including any work related to linking the image to the text.

The coordinator of digital graphics is the person responsible for cataloguing all digitized images. It may be useful to use external software, in addition to the database, such as supplementary programs that aid in media management, for example, ACDSee or Cumulus.

Many objects are scanned for publication in the museum catalogues, magazines, and journals. Scans for the publications department are more often than not in Macintosh specification. Other scans may be in other digital formats. The coordinator of digital graphics is responsible for converting them to the unified standard and identifying each object with the help of the curator by a registration number. The coordinator of digital graphics also collects scans previously stored on various CDs and adds them to the stored scans on the server. This coordinator is in charge of the scanners and digital cameras in the museum.

For the curators, often the decision is to computerize retroactively all the catalogue cards for the curators' use, exactly as they exist in their handwritten form. The cards are not edited upon entry but entered exactly as they exist in their current form. On the registrar level, their ledgers should also be digitized and linked to the related digitized data. The mass of data that represents the objects must be broken down into basic elements and decisions must be made as to what data will reside in the database. Do all texts need to be edited, or should only the texts viewed by the public be edited? Do all images need to be graphically edited, or, again, does this only relate to the images viewed by the public? The answers to these questions will affect the work flow steps and, subsequently, their matching database fields. Most important, decisions made will affect the budget.

In large museums it has been determined that there are three levels of information, and therefore three levels of input are required: the curator, the registrar, and the public.[1] For the curators, often the decision is to computerize retroactively all the catalogue cards for the curators' use, exactly as they exist in their handwritten form (retroactive entry of bulk data is discussed in Time and Money Checks for Staff and in Appendix VII—Report of Experiments Recycling Data in the Museum). The cards are not edited upon entry, but entered exactly as they exist in their current form. On the registrar level, their ledgers should also be digitized and linked to the related digitized catalogue cards by way of their registration number. In addition, all published exhibition labels should be linked in the same manner. The information viewed by the public requires translation and editing before publication and therefore is the most time-consuming and costly. In most institutions between 10 and 15 percent of the collections are exhibited and require this expensive treatment.

After determining which objects will be dealt with and how, the next step is to ascertain which staff will be responsible for inputting the information into the computer, at what stage, in what form, and at what level of quality. The enormous job of computerizing the entire collection of the museum requires typing, scanning, and processing of all the information, so there are many types of staff needed. To define the data entry staff, a list of required tasks, and hence job descriptions, must be constructed. The staff that fulfills these tasks may be current members or newly hired; these jobs can be done in-house, or they can be outsourced. This may include a typist, editor, and translator for multilingual textual information (one per language) and a person to do scanning and graphic artist.

Once staff and jobs are decided upon, as well as the quantity and type of data they will work with, it becomes possible to calculate the time and personnel necessary to insert this data into a database, and to budget for people and hours.

The data entry project can be estimated in terms of time and money by analyzing the amount of data related to each object, breaking the project into tasks, timing each task for an average object, and then estimating how much time and money the entire project will cost. Once the tasks have been defined, it is recommended to check the cost-efficiency of outsourcing versus in-house. When considering the digitization of large amounts of data (e.g., retroactively cataloguing entire collections), it is wise to consider outsourcing the work. When weighing the pros and cons of the costs and time involved in these two options, it must be taken into account that a member of the in-house staff will need to review the information entered by outsourced staff to affirm its quality. The resulting comparative information of outsourced and in-house will be the basis of all your budgeting for the computerization project, as 80 percent of costs are tied to personnel while the other 20 percent are connected with hardware and software.

In order to acquire a true price quote for an outsourced workforce, the project manager needs to compare apples to apples—in this case clearly define the amount of text and the size of images required per object. To quantify the contents related to one object and to price an hour's work, some museums have used the principle that an object is well catalogued when described with

TABLE 5.1   Time and cost analysis for a multilingual computerization project (Assume that all the staff receives an average salary of $10 per hour.)

	Time in Minutes per Object	Cost in Dollars per Object	Total Time in Hours for 250,000 Objects	Total Time in Years for 250,000 Objects	Total Cost in Dollars for 250,000 Objects	Number of People Required for 10 Years for 250,000 Objects
Typist—Primary Language	15	3	62,500	39	625,000	4
Typist—Secondary Language*	15	3	6,250	4	62,500	0.5
Primary Language Editor	24	4	100,000	63	1,000,000	6
Secondary Language Editor*	24	4	10,000	6	100,000	0.5
Translator*	60	10	25,000	16	250,000	2
Scanner**	6	2	25,000	16	250,000	2
Scan Editor**	30	6	125,000	80	1,250,000	8
Team Managers***	n/a	n/a	63,360	10	633,600	3
Total	**174**	**32**	**417,110**	**234******	**4,171,100**	**26**

n/a = not applicable.
*As translating is time-consuming and expensive, it was decided that only the exhibited objects would have bilingual texts, and therefore only 10 percent of the collection's objects would be translated.
**Two pictures per object on average.
***One team manager per group of workers (one in charge of the primary language staff, one for the secondary language staff and one for the digital image staff).
****Total years of personnel.

an average of one page of text (288 words) and two images each of 5MB. For a comparative table assembled from many museums, see Willpower Information Management Consultants, "Time Taken to Create Catalogue Records for Museum Objects," http://www.willpowerinfo.co.uk/. Another valuable source of information can be found in Appendix E of "Scoping the Future of the University of Oxford Digital Library Collections: Funded by the Andrew W. Mellon Foundation—Final Report," http://www.bodley.ox.ac.uk/scoping /report.html. In this section Stuart D. Lee details the main issues in the digitization chain. Although it was published in 1999, it is still a valid work, illuminating the topic in a comprehensive manner.[2]

Table 5.1 formulates a museum staffing budget for a project in which 250,000 objects are to be digitized in a bilingual format, with images.

From Table 5.1 we can see that a project of this scope would cost a museum over $4 million in workforce alone, and over ten years to complete with a staff of 26 people. In simpler terms it would take 234 years for one person to complete this project!

The disadvantage of the table compiled is that the estimate for the 250,000 objects' input time does not include rest, vacations, lunch, sick days, overhead, and so on. The staff input was determined and the final estimation calculated as if the staff was a machine that was working nonstop. In essence it was necessary to add additional time to the calculations—up to 25 percent more than the original estimates.

A large staff is necessary to implement this project. Therefore, the location of the staff members becomes a central issue as staff must be not only hired but also given space to work. For this reason another calculation is required to ascertain which members of staff could remain on the museum campus. The following considerations can be taken into account:

- The source material must not leave the museum grounds.
- The worker should have direct access to curators and others in charge of data.
- The work should be done in a time frame that can be monitored.

In order to solve some of these problems, it may be decided that all persons who work with source data—that is, index cards or photographs—will work on the museum grounds, and all who work with digital files, that is, the translators, editors, and graphic editor, can work off-campus. (For more on this topic, see Appropriate Handling of Original Material in chapter 7). The graphic editor may find it more difficult to work off-campus, however, as images can be in very large files and can be too cumbersome to relay back and forth. File sharing mechanism, for example, an FTP site, is one way of relaying information to off-site staff.

Each department should be asked to choose a representative to present its needs. Understanding computers and how databases work are important criteria when appointing the liaison. This staff member will first assemble and help define and coordinate all relevant material. The liaison's tasks include:

- Defining field names and their types
- Creating lexicon lists
- Collecting report examples
- Collating all current departmental data by objects

There are two types of staff—existing and additional. The existing staff and curators are the key to data entry. They have all the information, are often the same ones who handwrite the catalogue cards, and are familiar with the whereabouts of the object's current information. It is unfortunate that many curators are not interested in typing in their entire collection, yet they hold the key to the information. It is possible to release the data (i.e., catalogue cards, original images) from the museum so that an outsourced typist can type and scan all the data. A compromise would be to hire a typist who would sit in the department and have access to the information and also to the person who wrote the information. This would allow the most accurate input of data at the lowest cost. The curators' time for answering these questions and later reviewing all entries must be budgeted. Only objects that have been approved by a curator can be viewed in the database. In reference to the large quantity of staff required for this project, many museums have found it worthwhile and cost-effective to retrain current staff and to involve them in the project as it develops.

HARDWARE AND SOFTWARE

A server is necessary to store all the data. IBM's DB2, Oracle, or Microsoft SQL Server are the main choices for a server. They provide powerful servers with additional memory available in modular units. The institution should take into consideration when making its choice the available local support for each company as well as the costs. Some servers have more experience than others with specific languages involved (including Semitic languages). Aside from the initial purchase costs, a museum must be aware that upkeep of a server requires funds, including licensing fees, backup mechanisms, and in some cases a full time database administrator (DBA).

SERVER AND BACKUPS

It is important to consider how much space will be necessary for the images, which are very large. It is wise to budget an average size of 5 MB per image. At this minimum size, it can be concluded that if the initial server space of 17 GB costs $8,000 it would cost the institution to store an image approximately $2 with an additional $0.5 a year for backup tapes. These costs do not include the additional necessity of off-site backup. For more on preservation of digital information, see the section entitled Long-Term Storage Solutions in chapter 7.

NOTES

1. Allison Siffre Guedalia Kupietzky, "Computerization of Encyclopedic Museum Collections: A Case Study Addressing the Special Multilingual Challenges of a Semitic Language Museum" (PhD diss., The Union Institute and University, Cincinnati, Ohio, 2004).
2. The topic of cost reduction and cost efficiency is broached by Simon Tanner and Marilyn Deegan, "Exploring Charging Models for Digital Cultural Heritage: Digital Image Resource Cost Efficiency and Income Generation Compared with Analog Resources. A HEDS Report" (New York: Andrew W. Mellon Foundation, 2002). Another source is Minerva Europe, Identification of Good Practices and Competence Centers Working Group, "Digitisation Cycle Cost Reduction," http://www.minervaeurope.org/structure/working groups/goodpract/costreduction/documents/wp6costreduction0904.pdf.

CHAPTER 6

Step 4: Analyzing Needs

UNDERSTANDING THE WORK FLOW OF THE MUSEUM

When approaching the task of computerizing the objects, the project manager should first inspect the institution's work habits: the forms filled out (input of information) and the reports mailed out (output of information). Examples of forms and reports include catalogue cards, condition reports, shipping documentation, and so on. These forms and reports help to show which fields are used by the museum staff.

UNIFYING THE MUSEUM

Large museums consist of many different departments, each of which works autonomously. In order to enjoy the full capabilities of the database, it falls on the administration to unify the museum under the umbrella of one program. To do this, a global needs analysis of the museum's needs, departmental needs, and personal work habits should be compiled. There is flexibility in most database programs that allows each user to customize the fields and reports to suit individual work habits. This allows the museum to unify the process and the fields used by everyone. The project manager should be able to make use of the database flexibility and to customize the user's screen to reflect personal needs or preferences.

DEFINING THE DEPARTMENTS

The museum's project manager should list all the curatorial and service departments that would benefit from a Collections Management Database System. In most museums, the database is built in accordance with the curators' needs, for their needs are the most complex, and their cataloguing needs require specialized data fields. It is the curator's role to manage the collections and their pertinent information. There is supplementary data for each object, which comes via the service departments (publishing, exhibit design department, rights and reproductions, photography of collections department, etc.). All these data may become too cumbersome to manage. The project manager should decide the scope of the data to be included in the program.

Although the curators are the prime clients for database input and output, one should not overlook the needs of the public and the museum's goal of sharing this information. In the long term work flow, the data should be accessible to the public, and this goal should guide the data input at the early stages. For example, the artist's dates of birth and death may not be pertinent to the curators on a daily basis but should be accessible in a public Web site. On the other hand, an anonymous donor's name should not be made public at any point in the work flow so as to safeguard the donor's identity.

NEEDS ANALYSIS OF USERS

In order to fully understand the work flow of a museum, it is necessary to interview each end user. In the interviews it is important to determine what the user does in the museum, how the database can assist the user, and what this user expects to achieve by utilizing the database system. A work flow analysis and needs analysis summarize this. It is best done with the help of a computer company, as it will be able to translate the work flow and the associated activities into fields that meet these needs.

WORK FLOW—WHO DOES WHAT

The following example demonstrates the journey an object takes through the museum and the staff involved in this process.

1. The object arrives at the museum via the guard.
2. The object is photographed and a digital image produced; a temporary number is assigned to the object and its image file name. The object is placed in a storage closet until "stage 5" (fields: registered by, date of registration, authority: registrar, level 1).
3. The initial registration number is given to the object and the digital image is connected to the text (fields: department number, object, origin, date, artist, material, technique, donor, registered by, date of registration, authority: curator, level 1).
4. The object is assigned a final accession number. Text and image file names are amended (fields: registered by, date of registration, authority: registrar, level 2).
5. Information is added during the cataloguing process (fields: size, provenance, storage place, descriptive text, see also, registered by, date of registration, authority: curator, level 2).
6. The exhibition stage includes amending the associated fields (fields: movement of object, bibliography, museum negative number, multimedia file, photographer, credit, registered by, date of registration, authority: curator, level 3).

Note that the field names used do not follow the Getty format. For a full list of CDWA field names, see "Categories for the Description of Works of Art (CDWA)."[1]

At each stage, the staff member assigned to the task is noted, along with his/her authorization level. The authorization level can include one or all of the following options in regard to data: not to see, to see, to write, to erase. When two people work on the same field, it is important to have the option of "locking" fields so that one does not overwrite the other. Another way to ensure security of information is to make use of a database log which should register every change or addition to the database, who did it and when.

AUTHORIZATIONS

It is essential to analyze the staff authorized to access classified information in the museum. Can the registrar see all the details the curator can see? What information can the public access from the database?

The topic of public access to museum information is explored in depth by the Archives & Museum Informatics site (www.archimuse.com). This site lists many articles relating to this complex topic. Special emphasis is placed on enabling educational use of digital museum collections.[2] One of the immediate options with the browser is that the information can be made available to all the curators as well as the public. It is important that the curators understand all the capabilities and limitations of the system. In the case of large museums five levels of users have been defined:

1. The Public. The museum should have some objects accessible to the public (people who "visit" the museum outside the museum's walls) on the Internet to search as well as browse in a virtual collection (e.g., for a list of Web sites see Appendix VIII—Fifteen Worldwide Museum Sites Reviewed). (Data output: text in twelve fields, thumbnail of image.)
2. Visitors. The museum should allow access to visitors (people who physically visit the museum) via an Intranet, which is an internal network. (Data output: text in twelve fields, thumbnail of image, may include other cumbersome multimedia, e.g., videos.)
3. Curators and Administrators (including the curatorial service departments). Other museum staff members or those not in charge of that specific object in the museum should have access to an Intranet combining thumbnails and labels of all digitized information. (Data output: text in twelve fields, thumbnail of image.)
4. The Registrar. The registrar should have access to the information that relates to the cataloguing of objects and a thumbnail image. (Data input and output: text in twenty-four fields, thumbnail of image.)
5. The Curator. Only the curator should have complete access to the high-resolution images and the full body of texts. (Data input and output: text in seventy-two fields, archival/high resolution image.) There are many variables to consider when choosing the guidelines for image resolution. These include storage space and final distribution modes among other issues. In the article titled "High Resolution Digital Image Storage at the National Railway Museum, York" some of these issues are discussed by Ben Booth and Christine J. Heap.[3]

ANALYSIS OF THE BASIC MUSEUM MANAGEMENT PROGRAM

It is important that the baseline program fulfills elementary criteria in order to enable proper museum collection management.

The program should have the ability to handle the language or languages used in cataloguing the objects. Museums, which have to cater to a multilingual public, need a program that has the ability to conform to the writing standards of each language simultaneously. Chinese-Japanese-Korean (CJK) languages pose certain challenges in the digitization process, but they run left to right like western languages and therefore do not have to deal with bidirectionality (e.g., see Hong Kong Heritage Museum, www.heritagemuseum .gov.hk). Semitic languages are the most challenging as they run from right to left. The interfacing must be bidirectional in order to host both Semitic and western languages.

Each collection has different needs with regard to fields. There are many fields that overlap between any two collections, but there are also many unique to each collection. For example, an archaeology collection would use the fields "material" and "site" while a fine arts collection would use the fields "material" and "artist." Because the work needs evolve, the ability to add new fields in the program is important.

As the needs of a museum change with time, the flexibility with regard to fields—the ability to add new fields, change the names of current fields, and so on—is important. Sarasan stresses that "any system must allow for the extension or revision of the data standard to incorporate new or changed categories, as it is not always possible to anticipate future requirements."[4]

There are four basic text field types:

1. Free text fields can contain as many words as necessary in any language. Example: **Description** field: "A Pair of Silver Candlesticks, fluted columns on loaded base."
2. Numerical or alphanumeric fields can contain numbers, dates, or letters (if alphanumeric) and do not need to be translated in a multilingual database. Example: **Registration number** field: "B1234.0022."
3. Drop-down list or lexicon fields. This is a controlled terminology list; terms may be obtained by typing the first letter. A lexicon field often has a hierarchical tree of associated words. Example: **Origin** field: "Augsburg, Germany"; example: **Medium and Technique** field: "Silver, repoussé."
4. Yes/no fields. Example: **Can This Item Be Shown on the Internet** field: "Yes."

A free text field is not a controlled field as opposed to a list or lexicon field. It contains text, such as an item description. This can include many words in many languages (Unicode allows for multilingualism). For efficient retrieval, it is best not to rely too much on this kind of field, because the computer will have to search every word to come up with results. For this reason it is better to rely more on controlled terminology found in the list or lexicon field. As there is a limit to the amount of text a free text field can contain, it is best to check this before assuming that all long descriptive strings can fit in this field.

The text field can either be a "string field" with a limitation, for example, in Microsoft Access of 255 characters, or a "memo field" with no limitation in Microsoft Access but a limitation prescribed by the database (e.g., Oracle) of 10,000 characters. A fixed length field may contain from 0 to 255, while a text field may contain from 0 to 32,000 characters (limit depends on the variable declaration).

Numerical fields contain only numbers. A year field could be a numeric field. But if you require a full date or an approximate date (circa 1950), then you need to use an alphanumeric field. An alphanumeric field can contain any data, including numbers. However, when an alphanumeric field does contain texts and numbers, it cannot be used as a number nor can it be sorted or searched in a range (e.g., a query on a range of years: "find all works from 1940 to 1960"). In most cases, in a multilingual database system it, it is unnecessary to translate numeric fields, such as those containing dates or registration numbers.

Drop-down alternatives (of words) appear in both primary and secondary languages in a multilingual database system and can have optional terms expanded, which are in turn listed alphabetically. There may be one language in the input screen, which will determine the alphabetization to which the parallel translation is attached. When typing the first letter, the word closest to this letter should appear. The fields need a basic list that can be added to over time. If this list is prepared in advance, it might speed up the input process and increase the efficiency of the program. Searches will be streamlined, as the search will be based on a set list of choices. In lexicon fields a term is part of a tree or hierarchy of associations. "Jerusalem," for example, is the name of cities in many states and countries. When searching for the word Jerusalem, one would be given a choice of such countries and, in the end, could choose, for example, Jerusalem, New Jersey, USA. Another characteristic of these fields is that they enable the user to associate synonymous terms to a word (e.g., Lvov = Lemberg). This field type is useful when searching hierarchical information, which can be accessed via either broad terms or parent terms. For example, the field titled "State" is the parent term for many cities. When searching for the state of New Jersey, the search results would include everything below that branch of the word tree—in this case cities— that is, Jerusalem, Teaneck, Newark, and so on.

Yes/no fields are limited to a question that can be answered with a negative or positive response.

Once these field types are understood, their definitions can be chosen and applied to the correct data. The first task is to list the fields in which data will be placed, name them, and then choose the type of field suitable. In addition, a list of frequently used terms for the "drop-down fields" specific for each department needs to be compiled. The lists must be formulated, translated, and edited, ensuring that as soon as the field content is chosen in the primary language, the secondary language correlation will appear. These lists should be viewed as a skeleton for later additions, because as more data are added these lists will grow. Only a senior curator should approve these additions and have them officially translated and edited so that the integrity of the program is maintained.

In addition to text fields there will be data associated with multimedia—images, audio, movies, and so on. The program should allow the user to view the image up close or from afar (zoom in and out). The initial screen viewing of each object should include a thumbnail image and a short descriptive text. The program should be able to link other media, including Adobe PDF files. The ability to link allows the insertion of ancient texts or hieroglyphics.

Images can come from scanning photos, slides, catalogues, and negatives. In addition a digital camera can be used as an initial documenting tool to take a "passport picture" of the objects as they enter the museum. These images are for identifying the object visually, but not for publications (i.e., catalogues, Internet, kiosks, CDs, etc.).

In many countries there are stipulations regarding the care of national treasures and what information needs to be catalogued for these objects. For example, in Israel there is a museum law that requires each object to be catalogued with a textual description and an analogue photo documenting its existence.[5] While computerizing the collections, some catalogued objects may be found without an image. These discrepancies will come to light and can be corrected during digitization.

It should be possible to fine-tune access to the data within the program. There should be systems of authorizations to allow access for each level of user, for example, curator, registrar, and public. The curators will be able to enter information that is privileged or confidential (e.g., the name of an anonymous donor). The flexibility of authorization should be on a user-name level and include the ability to define the specific fields accessible to each user. (For specific examples, see the heading titled Authorizations earlier in this chapter.)

The search mechanism should be easy to use and support searches in all languages found in the program. It should be possible to perform a search on part of a word, and in more complicated systems according to the phonetic properties. The user should be able to search the lexicon and free text fields. Multicriteria and Boolean searches should be available.

The user should be able to generate reports by different criteria according to different requirements and include multilingual capabilities and images. The user should be able to save the reports and to create templates in a flexible and easy manner. For example, in a catalogue card printed using a report template, the data would be retrieved from the database, the template would be formatted so that all the fields can fit onto the size of the paper index cards used in the printer, and an image should be printed out as well. A report containing a large image and a label can be generated directly from the database or using an external report program, such as Crystal Report and Business Objects. The report should be able to be saved in open and closed file formats such as Rich Text File, HTML, or Adobe PDF. (See Figure 6.1)

Examples of reports might include printouts of digitized catalogue cards, condition reports, shipping documentation, and so on.

FIGURE 6.1   An example of a business objects report containing a large image and a label saved as a PDF file

Fruitmeisje (Fruitseller). c. 1916. No signature, entitled on reverse.
Oil on canvas. 36 x 50 cm.   Cat. 208.

The program should enable the user to upload data directly from the database system into HTML in such a way that would be viewable from a browser. The data could be exported on-the-fly, in a dynamic format, or it could be static. The viewer should be able to see texts and images, in both high and low resolution.

NOTES

1. For a definition, see Murtha Baca and Patricia Harpring, "List of Categories and Definitions," http://www.getty.edu/research/conducting_research/stand ards/cdwa/8_printing_options/definitions.pdf.
2. For a listing of publications, see Archives & Museum Informatics, "Articles and Papers," http://www.archimuse.com/publishing/papers.html.
3. Ben Booth and Christine J. Heap. "High Resolution Digital Image Storage at the National Railway Museum, York," in *Museums and Interactive Multimedia*, ed. Diane Lees (Cambridge, UK: Museum Documentation Association, 1993), 1–5.
4. Lenore Sarasan, "Why Museum Computer Projects Fail." *Museum News 59* no. 4 (January–February 1981): 40–49.
5. Only recently the role of museums in Israel has been defined, and with the increase in the number of museums has come a greater need to create a system for supervision and training to guide continuity and development. In 1975, the

Ministry of Education and Culture appointed a special commission to study museums in Israel. Its work led to the Passage of Museums Act (1983) and Museum Regulations Act (1984), which set standards for museum operations and personal training. In 1993, thirty-four Israeli museums were recognized under the museum acts, and museums studies' programs offering professional training for museums' personnel are being developed. Judith Inbar, "On the History and Nature of Museums in Israel," in *Museums and the Needs of People* (CECA Conference, Jerusalem, Israel, October 15–22, 1991), 15–22.

CHAPTER 7

Step 5: Standardizing Data in the Most Efficient Manner—Image, Text, and Multimedia

DEFINING DATA

A database contains digitized information. The source of this information can be nondigital (printed catalogues, catalogue cards, etc.) or digital (computer files of three types: images, texts, and other multimedia). Each type of data has its own issues that need to be resolved.

IMAGES—QUALITY AND STORAGE

The purpose for which the digitized images will be used will define the quality of the image required. Print quality is acceptable for books and catalogues,

FIGURE 7.1 Example of a final label from the Online Collections of the American Museum of Natural History

POTTERY BOWL, DECORATED [H/15170]
Culture: HOPI (MOKI)
Locale: AZ, NAVAJO COUNTY, HOPI INDIAN RESERVATION,
    FIRST MESA VICINITY
Country: USA
Material: CLAY, PIGMENT
Dimensions: D:17.7 H:9 RIM:16.7
Donor: HRDLICKA, ALES, DR. Accession No: 1900-51

See Appendix IX for an example of a digitized collection for more information on the Online Collections of the American Museum of Natural History recommended at up to 600 dpi (dots per inch), screen usage with a zoom-in capability requires 300 dpi, thumbnails average 72 dpi for Internet or identification purposes. In a best practice situation, it is recommended to store the noncompressed highest resolution your institution can afford as an archival image but access on a daily basis a low-resolution thumbnail. In most databases this thumbnail can be viewed on the screen and the archival version accessed by "double clicking" on the thumbnail. This makes searching much less cumbersome and time-consuming.

Accumulated scans need to be stored. The most efficient form of storage is on hard drives, allowing immediate access to images. If space does not permit this, it is recommended to use CDs or DVDs. Ideally all images should be stored together in a certain order, using a consistent tag (e.g., an accession number). (For more on long-term storage preservation, see the section in the chapter titled Long-Term Storage Solutions.)

TEXTS—QUALITY AND STORAGE

In the museum there are many levels of quality for a text. It begins its life at the curator's desk as a personal note describing an image and finally is presented to the public as a concise and edited text.

Before a text is presented to the public it passes through many hands:

1. An assistant curator/intern supplies the basic facts related to the object.
2. A curator adds a full description.
3. An editor reviews the text and makes necessary corrections.
4. A curator approves corrections.
5. Corrections are incorporated.
6. An editor/translator adds the complementary language.
7. A curator approves the translation.
8. A copy editor reviews both texts and marks necessary corrections.
9. A curator approves corrections.
10. Corrections are incorporated.

A final label example may read as follows:

A Pair of Silver Candlesticks

Germany, 19th Century
Silver, repoussé
H:5, Diam: 8.9 cm
Our Museum Collection
Purchased and donated by Steve and Ruth Klein, Cleveland, 1969
Registration number: 1234.56

The collections database team's goal is to store all texts in a database attaching the texts as a single unique object. These texts are tagged by using the object's unique number (i.e., the registrar or accession number). A prose text that is recorded in a consistent readable format can be converted into data for fields in a database. This allows them to be searched efficiently. This also would avoid the need to repeatedly type the texts. Texts that already exist in fields or in a tabular format are easiest to convert and incorporate into a database. This is because all databases consist of information saved in tables or columns, in the back-end. This is often referred to as ODBC—Open Data Base Connectivity. (For more information on Long-Term Storage Solutions, see the section in this chapter.)

MULTIMEDIA—QUALITY AND STORAGE

Multimedia can include many formats: videos, sound tracks, catalogue images, and so on. These might include sound, movies, and hyperlinks. All available museum media that are juxtaposed with historical, religious, or contextual associations, add dimensions to the object. The rights to all these must either belong to the museum or be secured so that the media can be shown to the public. Tony Gill in *The MDA Guide to Computers in Museums* defines multimedia and lists many of its current permutations in chapter four.[1] (For more on long-term storage preservation, see the section titled Long-Term Storage Solutions in this chapter.)

USERS DEFINED

The interfacing of the program should reflect the users' needs: Are they curators or visitors? Are they Hebrew-speaking Israeli students or researchers who are more comfortable in English? Will the program be used by the general public? If so, it must be very straightforward with few instructions and places to get lost. Will it be used by curators who are trained to use the database for specific tasks? Each department will have different needs with regard to the program's interfacing.

In the museum world there are three levels of front-end users, which can be defined as follows:

1. Low level. Passersby with a short attention span needing a fully guided search with objects in clearly organized and defined groups.
2. Medium level. Semiguided searches with a longer attention span, for example, students with the goal of organizing objects into groups.
3. High level. In-depth study, including complex queries leading to new information and categories.

Back-end or data entry museum staff are defined as follows:

1. Basic input level (secretarial). Input of prepared material.
2. Medium level (editorial). Editing of source material.
3. High level (curators). Input of original material.

SOURCE MATERIAL FOR DIGITIZATION

When considering the many formats of source material—texts, images, video or audio files—the following aspects need to be examined: data type, cataloguing system, users, and notes pertaining to the data (referred to as meta-data). There are many sources of material or data stored within the walls of the museum. Source material, or original material, can be defined as pretyped texts and prescanned images; refined data can be defined as typed or edited texts, scanned or digitized images. The source material can be divided into those created for staff and those used for public viewing, for example, publications.

The type of images, texts, and other multimedia found in the museum can be categorized by who produces them, where they are stored, and how they are catalogued. In order to unify the standard of these data, it is highly recommended to construct guidelines for the process. To construct these guidelines, one can review guidelines found in similar institutions. An example of a comprehensive set of guidelines can be seen in "Digital Imaging and Preservation Microfilm: The Future of the Hybrid Approach for the Preservation of Brittle Books."[2] See below for an example of museum guidelines. This example is a recommended set of guidelines that has evolved after working on the computerization project at the Israel Museum, Jerusalem.

GUIDELINES FOR THE DIGITIZATION OF TEXTS AND IMAGES

Example of Museum's Guidelines for the Digitization of Texts and Images

UNIFYING CURRENT DATA—PREPARING FOR INSERTION INTO DATABASE

Media will be identified and unified in format (for PC) so that all previously completed works that are saved in a museum (or at publishing houses) can be accessed and broken down into their various principle elements of pictures, audio, video, and texts. Information to be included in this stage should include past digitized publications, labels, videos, and image and audio files.

Each multimedia file needs to be divided into multiple files, which reflect the objects they address. These will be saved and given the name of the object's registration number.

Image files should be saved as tiff and catalogued in Cumulus. The addition of a running number to the file name will be added to multiple scans of the same object.

Texts can be saved as "notes" and be accessible via the image files found in Cumulus. Alternatively they can be saved as Word files according to the registration number.

All video and audio files should also be saved according to the registration number and catalogued in an image-cataloguing program (like Cumulus by Canto).

In the final database, all the above elements will be linked together.

SCANNING GUIDELINES

The range of image quality starts with objects, which have not been photographed to those with high-resolution scans. When computerizing the collection, a museum's intention is to have at least one image scanned per object. There are two options: either to digitize the object's image that exists on the catalogue cards at this time or to obtain or create a high-quality image of the object (published catalogue, slide, or digital camera image). The curator's role is to help determine which images will represent the object in the database.

GUIDELINES FOR DIGITIZING IMAGES

(In order of low- to high-range image)

If no image exists, take conventional and digital photographs simultaneously.
If a black-and-white image exists, scan that photo or do as above.
If a color contact exists, scan it.
If a transparency exists, scan it.
Once scanned, assign the object a file name, which will reflect its registration number.
Give it an additional sequential number to denote its number scan.

As file names require specific punctuation, the periods (.) should be changed to underscores (_) and the tilde (̃) will be used to separate the registration number from the running number (e.g., 2000_1_12341).

TARGET RESOLUTION AND SAVING INSTRUCTIONS

The recommended target high resolution should be 1500×2100 or 300 dpi of a $5\times7''$. Save as a tiff file. Store images directly onto the server in departmental folders.

CONNECTING IMAGES TO TEXTS

One of the most important tasks is the connection of descriptive texts to the images. Scans should not be done for unidentified images. Each scan file must be saved with a number that relates it to the item's registration number. The curators can identify, assemble, and connect the images to the catalogue cards. As this is a lengthy process, a team of volunteers working under the guidance of curators can assist in this task.

In case the curators were not able to find time for this, small black-and-white images found on the catalogue cards can be used with the long-term goal of improving the image in the future (either by rephotographing the work with a digital camera or finding a better image in a published catalogue).

TEXT GUIDELINES

The text quality can be edited for three uses: internal use (curatorial or departmental use), staff use (administrative or registrar use), and external use (texts which have been prepared for "public consumption"). These texts are edited and translated.

Most of the texts found in museums are unstructured and need to be broken down into information that can fit into specific database fields. This task may be given to a data inputter with the ability to ascertain which texts should go into each field (artist name, place, etc.) and which texts are for internal or public consumption.

GUIDELINES FOR DIGITIZING TEXTS

The goal in digitizing is to mirror the current situation in a museum. It will not be possible to compare or upgrade the data for each object in the museum before digitization (this would take years), and so a decision has to be made to digitize what exists (computerized or handwritten).

The database will have a PC (personal computer) interfacing and so one of the challenges is in unifying the platform of the texts that come from outside sources. This is particularly a challenge with the Hebrew texts containing formatting codes, which get lost in the transfer from Macintosh to a PC compatible platform. The data entered should come from the curator's catalogue cards, as this will be the basis for all data pertaining to the object. For the sake of efficiency, the registrar's database will be supplemented by the curator's information found in their handwritten catalogue cards. In addition, as publications continue to be produced it is important that curators request this digital information back from the publishing house.

Data are taken from three prime sources:

1. The curator's catalogue cards (handwritten).
2. The registrar's books (handwritten, typed, or computerized).
3. The labels or other publications for an item (curators should request this information to be saved onto a CD at the end of the publication process).

ANCIENT TEXTS AND HIEROGLYPHICS

One of the challenges in typing in the texts from the handwritten cards is how to input ancient texts and hieroglyphics. The solution is to type the texts into a Word document with the file name equivalent to the registration number for the object so that it can be linked to the object in the database or to scan the image of the ancient text and save it as you would an image. This is also applicable to hand-drawn sketches of inscriptions or hallmarks. These supplementary documents should be saved alongside the images on the server to be connected to the object at a later date in the database (assistance and training by the collection management staff is available).

LEXICON

The lexicon plays an essential role in the uniformity of the museum's terms used in the database. A lexicon is a tree of words placed in a hierarchical format. The words are placed within branches with each word defined as the primary, alternate, or relational term to the next. The lexicon is unique to each collection/museum and is built over time. The museum's personal lexicon is built based on "legacy terms" (terms in use in the museum today). Because some departments work in a number of languages, the lexicon is multilingual.

In the database some fields are lexicon dependent.

When entering a term, the cataloguer must perform a search to determine that the term does not already exist in the lexicon.

If a new term must be entered, it should be translated to the secondary language at the same time. This will enable the lexicon to fill in and store the term in the secondary language with regard to bilingual terms.

Any user may enter a new term into the lexicon. The registrar's office is in charge of quality assurance, and a term not edited by them will appear in the lexicon as red. The red terms should be used with caution, as they have not yet been approved

New terms should be translated immediately upon input. This is because the database requires both language terms for the translating feature to work.

All new words are reviewed regularly (once a month) by a professional team of translators and editors.

Terms that are not accepted may be changed by the registrar's office only after consulting with the curators. They will then be updated by a batch change in the database using the corrected terms but leaving the curators' terms as secondary alternatives.

The lexicon team follows the guidelines prescribed by the Getty index. (See http://www.getty.edu/research/conducting_research/vocabularies/aat/faq.html.)

The controlled terms found in the lexicon can perform a number of tasks. The lexicon can translate terms in the database, as well as aid in searches and help perform batch changes.

When a term is selected in either the primary language or the secondary language, the lexicon chooses the complementary term in the opposing language. That is, if a typist working in the Judaica department inputs the Hebrew word "חרוט" for technique, the lexicon will fill in the English term "engraved" in the appropriate field.

The lexicon constitutes the backbone of an elaborate search mechanism for misspelled words, alternative spellings, synonyms, and broad and narrow terms. For example, if one were to search for "Piccaso," the lexicon would recognize the term as an alternate term (even if misspelled) for the primary word "Picasso." The computer would then locate all objects with this term. In addition, if one would search for the broad term "cubist artists," Picasso (the narrow term) would appear along with other cubist artists.

The lexicon aids in searches for synonyms and alternates. A dictionary is linear, but a lexicon is built in a hierarchical manner allowing words to be associated with each other as broader, narrower, synonymous, or related terms. This important tool allows the computer to recognize various words and their synonyms. For example, "Lvov" and "Lemberg" refer to the same place at different points of time. Using a lexicon, a person will be able to search for Lvov and find information about objects associated with the city of Lemberg.

The lexicon can help identify additional information about an ambiguous term in a scope note. Scope notes serve two basic purposes: to clarify the precise meanings of concepts and to advise on usage. For example, two artists can have the same name. When choosing the artist, the dates of birth and death of each term can be consulted in the scope notes, and then the relevant person can be chosen. To illustrate this point: when searching for Hans Holbein, an artist who lived during the Renaissance, two artists lived in the fifteenth century by that name, yet one lived from 1465–1524 and the other from 1497–1543.

Updating the words can be done via the lexicon globally, as a batch update. For example, Paris was transliterated in Hebrew with the equivalent of an "s" in the 1980s and today with the equivalent of a "z." A change of this type can be made in the lexicon term and will affect all objects described using this term.

APPROPRIATE HANDLING OF ORIGINAL MATERIAL

In many cases, the source material is rare or valuable, and the negative effect of digitization on the source material needs to be minimized. Treating the originals with care refers both to the preparation of these materials for digitization, for example when removing the frame of a painting, and during the process of digitization, for example when placing an object on a scanner. The specialist knowledge of the individuals who are responsible for the source material on a day-to-day basis will be valuable to the project team. Those responsible for the project must weigh the risks of exposing original material to any digitization process, especially where the items are unique, valuable, or fragile, and must discuss the process with those responsible for the care of the originals. It might be recommended that the items be handled only with gloves or under certain physical conditions, for example, low temperatures, dim lighting.[3] This affects the cost for handling intrinsic to the medium of the originals. Large items such as maps and fragile materials such as glass or photographs will require more time and effort to handle when moving the original onto the scan mechanism. In order to reduce the risk of damaging the item, it sometimes might be more appropriate to bring the camera, scanner, and so forth to the object rather than moving the object to the camera, scanner, and so forth. Other useful tips mentioned in the *Good Practice Handbook* include avoid unbinding of bound books and records, use of a scanner with a book cradle or a digital camera rather than a flatbed scanner, and the removal of staples, paper clips, and other fasteners as they can damage both the digitization devices and the source material.[4]

STAFF TRAINING AND COSTS

The project manager needs to ensure that all staff, in-house and/or outsourced, receives proper training in the use of digitization and software and in the appropriate handling of original materials. This will ensure that the process is efficient and that any risk to the originals is minimized.[5] Because more time is required for material needing special care, the cost is affected. A useful reference on this relationship between time and cost in the handling and digitization of material can be found in "The HEDS Matrix of Potential Cost Factors," http://heds.herts.ac.uk/resources/matrix.html. In addition, the University of Melbourne has published a useful guide to conservation, including the handling of fragile materials, at http://home.vicnet.net.au/~conserv/prepast1.htm.

USE AND REUSE

The use of information already in the museum, that is, texts and images, and input of this information into a database, will save the museum a large amount of money. Experiments conducted by the author using texts and images produced for other uses considered the reuse of digital and nondigital published information found in museums. The texts and images were considered recycled as they were originally produced for publication or as labels for an exhibition and not for use in a database. It is important to review these data in light of the guidelines for each type of information and not use data that do not fit the standards chosen for a particular database. (See the heading Source Material for Digitization in this chapter for more on this topic.)

Six experiments were performed—all with the intention of learning the most efficient manner of accumulating digitized information in a generic format for conversion to the final database. The goal was to investigate the most time and cost-efficient manner of acquiring digital information.

The experiments included:

1. Recycling edited and translated texts from texts produced for wall labels.
2. Recycling edited and translated texts from a Word document prepared for a multimedia exhibit.
3. Recycling images from scans and texts originally prepared for the publication of catalogues.
4. Using OCR (optical character recognition) for transferring information for a hard copy of a catalogue to a Word file.

5. Comparing the above to entering data straight from the catalogue cards.
6. Using Microsoft Access to turn tables on their axis.

To summarize the results: Experiments 1, 2, 3, 5, and 6 proved to be successful. Although in most cases the processes were time-consuming, the resulting information was high-quality data migrated into a new database format. This was not the case for experiment 4 where the OCR process resulted in very inaccurate data and did not have any advantages over rekeying the texts.

The conclusion and recommendation for the experiments are useful when approaching many different formats of previously created information. There was an 80 percent correction level of the secondary language from the image to the OCR text. A wrong letter in every five-letter word characterizes this percentage level. For this reason it is recommended to type in the information from scratch rather then use OCR. It was also concluded that the effort of tracking down the original texts was worthwhile. This was particularly true when dealing with edited and translated texts such as wall labels that often included tracking down the publisher who did the work in order to access the last version of the texts. (For a full review of the six experiments, see Appendix VII—Report of Experiments Recycling Data in the Museum.)

Throughout the curatorial wings and service departments of a museum, staff are scanning and archiving electronic images either with scanners or digital cameras. Volumes of texts are produced by the curatorial wings and processed through the publication, exhibition, and design departments, as well as by outside graphic designers. Analogue sound and video assets that can be digitized and archived are produced across museums in numerous departments and curatorial wings.

In order to prevent duplication and misuse of resources (e.g., image scans), the media management team manages the electronic assets through:

1. The provision of technical assistance to staff members who create electronic assets or who wish to digitize assets. These individuals are asked to save all new scans in a specific folder which is updated bimonthly by the collection database team using a media cataloguing system, like Cumulus. All users will be able to see the thumbnails of their files.
2. Creation and implementation of technical guidelines for images (guidelines for the scanning are set forth below).
3. Implementation of technical guidelines for texts.
4. Implementation of intellectual copyright guidelines.

LONG-TERM STORAGE SOLUTIONS

The storage of the data and the cataloguing system used in the database are very important elements to consider in the computerization process. "Preserving Digital Information: Report of the Task Force on Archiving of Digital Information" presents the clearest articulation of the problems associated with digital preservation, and galvanized a number of institutions and consortia both within the United States and abroad to consider the safekeeping and accessibility of digitized knowledge to be among their highest priorities.[6] Despite this attention, to date there is no universally agreed upon technological approach or institutional/consortia capability in place to guarantee continuing access to digitized materials of enduring value. Nonetheless, there are basic guiding principles that are agreed upon when considering long-term preservation of digital material: obsolescence, physical deterioration, and natural disaster. Attention to these issues is essential to digital preservation.[7]

OBSOLESCENCE

Avoiding obsolescence is the first principle when considering the format to be used for long-term storage of digital material. That is to say that the work produced during the digitization process will be rendered useless and unusable if it is not stored on up-to-date hardware and software. Different digital storage media have different software and hardware requirements for access, and different media present different storage and management challenges.

How to provide for long-term access should be considered from the planning stage when resources are being digitized (see the Calimera guidelines on digitization),[8] or from the creation stage in the case of "born digital" resources. It is useful to have a "life cycle" strategy that takes into account data creation, access policies, and preservation procedures, which is in place and ready to be applied before any images are captured.

FILE FORMATS

In the long term, the second important goal of any digitization project is to protect and keep accessible the data that it has created. This involves dealing with the inevitable obsolescence of digital file formats and various types of computer storage media. Preserving the digital master material and corresponding metadata helps to avoid having to redigitize any items, thus protecting the fragile source material and avoiding repetition of the labor-intensive digitization process including generating metadata.[9]

File format choice must be governed by the following principle: to create the highest quality digitization output and to make available migration paths for future preservation of the digital master. Saving the archival digitized material at the highest quality your institution can afford in the most generic format will help create a digital trail of data which can be reconstituted into a new format relatively easily. The role of standards in this area is very important. Before deciding on a file format, the relevant standards need to be taken into account. The more users a particular format has, the greater the likelihood the format will be supported in the future. Wide use of a format also indicates the likelihood of sustainable migration paths when file formats change. ERPANET suggests the following file formats for preservation:[10]

Text documents: plain ASCII, PDF, XML
Image documents: TIF, JPEG2000, JPEG
Audiovisual documents: WAV, BWF, MPEG

Proprietary file formats, that is, those requiring a privately owned software tool to open, and nonstandard media formats should be adopted only with great care. Bear in mind that all file formats and/or storage media will become obsolete in the foreseeable future (possibly less than five years, probably less than ten years). The size of the market for storage media provides an indication of how likely it is that migration from one medium to a new one will be feasible, as the medium becomes obsolete. If a proprietary solution is chosen, then there are dangers in its adoption, and project participants should be aware of the potential costs of this approach and should explore a migration strategy that will enable a future transition to open standards.[11]

TEXTUAL SCHEMA

In most cases storing text-based content in an SGML-or XML-based form conforming to a published Document Type Definition (DTD) or XML Schema will be the most appropriate option. Project participants need awareness of and understanding of the purpose of standardized formats for the encoding of texts, such as the Text Encoding Initiative (TEI), and should store text-based content in such formats when appropriate. Projects may store text-based content in SGML or XML formats conforming to other DTDs or schemas, but must provide mappings to a recognized schema. One should store these files in low-tech format so that the database can always be accessed and the data can be used; Open DataBase Connectivity (ODBC) not Oracle database would be recommended.

PHYSICAL DETERIORATION

If the shelf life of the file format is between five and ten years, then the hardware media chosen to preserve these digital files must be able to withstand the same test of time. CD-Rs and DVDs are within the means of all but the smallest projects; however, they do not replace magnetic tape media like Digital Linear Tape (DLT) as the storage medium of choice for backup of computer storage. There is conflicting opinion as to the longevity of these media, and there is no long-term research on this front.[12] Regardless of the choice of medium, it must be borne in mind that the medium will become obsolete in the future. Within five years, migration to new storage media is likely to be a necessity. Quoting Jeff Rothenberg, "Digital Information Lasts Forever, or Five Years, Whichever Comes First."[13]

There are three main technical approaches to digital preservation: technology preservation, technology emulation, and data migration. The first two focus on the technology used to access the object, either maintaining the original hardware and software or using current technology to replicate the original environment. Migration strategies focus on maintaining the digital objects in a form that is accessible using current technology. Such migrations may require the copying of the object from one medium or device to a new medium or device and/or the transformation of the object from one format to a new format.

NATURAL DISASTER

The third principle in digital preservation is the avoidance of natural disasters. Haven't you often heard the joke questioning the following preservation issue? In the case of an airplane crash, the black box survives intact in order to preserve the flights conversations and help the ground control understand why the crash occurred. Why can't the entire plane be made of the material used in the black box so they can ask the pilot himself?

While you cannot totally avoid natural disasters, by putting the multiple formats of material in many places, you can prevent them from affecting all of the copies of the material. Projects should consider creating copies of all their digital resources—metadata records as well as the digitized objects—on two different types of storage medium. At least one copy should be kept at a location other than the primary site to ensure that they are safe in the case of any disaster affecting the main site.

So if we can define a guiding principle to avoid data loss the material should be stored in three copies:

1. A hard copy, a printout
2. One backup stored on-site
3. One backup stored off-site

In addition, the material should be stored in two formats for backup besides the master digitized format. This can include backup disks from the servers and DVDs or other formats. For example, after digitizing a film on the hard drive, a VHS copy and DVD copy should be stored—one in California and one in India.

PRESERVATION COSTS

The cost of digitization projects is something that many cultural institutions are still struggling with, and there are problems inherent in the apportionment of fixed, variable, and "sunk" costs. Sunk costs include time of existing staff, premises, overheads, and so on. Other costs are unknown and to some extent unknowable (though reasonable assumptions can be made): costs of ongoing support and long-term preservation.[14] The choice of preservation strategy will be influenced by how authentic the preserved item needs to be. There is no universally accepted definition of authenticity, but it broadly means that the preserved copy should be as much like the original as possible, and the connections between documents and objects should be preserved to assist with interpretation.

Long-term preservation can be a costly exercise. To host an image on a server can cost up to $2 per 5 MB image in addition to a continuous backup on a tape that would cost $0.50 per year. Multiply this by as many objects as you have, and in the case of 20,000 items the cost would be a one time cost of $40,000 for server space and another $10,000 a year for backup tapes! In order to obtain a more "authentic" backup, you can employ a higher standard for the archival format. However, using the Getty Museum's standard for images, according to which each image size is closer to 65 MB, would involve twelve times the costs! (For a more detailed example, see the section titled Server and Backups in Chapter 5.)

NOTES

1. Tony Gill, *The MDA. Guide to Computers in Museums* (Cambridge, UK: Museum Documentation Association, 1996).
2. Stephen Chapman, Paul Conway, and Anne R. Kenney, Digital Imaging and Preservation Microfilm: The Future of the Hybrid Approach for the Preservation of Brittle Books, *RLG DigiNews* 3, no. 1 (February 15, 1999), http://www.clir.org/pubs/archives/hybrid.pdf#search='Digital%20Imaging%20and%20Preservation%20Microfilm%3A%20The%20Future%20of%20the%20Hybrid%20Approach%20for%20the%20Preservation%20of%20Brittle%20Books'.
3. "Joint RLG and NPO Preservation Conference Guidelines for Digital Imaging," 28–30 (The University of Warwick, September 28–30, 1998), http://www.rlg.org/preserv/joint/.
4. Minerva Working Group 6, ed., *Good Practice Handbook*, version 1.2, "Identification of Good Practices and Competence Centers" (Minerva Europe, November 2003), texts by Karl-Magnus Drake, Borje Justrell, and Anna Maria Tammaro, WP6 Secretariat: Marzia Piccininno.
5. TASI Web site, "Advice: Creating Digital Images," http://www.tasi.ac.uk/advice/creating/creating.html.
6. Research Libraries Groups, "Preserving Digital Information: Report of the Task Force on Archiving of Digital Information" (final report, Mountain View, California: RLG, May 1996), http://www.rlg.org/ArchTF/.
7. Recommended sources online: The AHDS provides a directory of material on the preservation of digital content at http://www.pads.ahds.ac.uk:81/padsProjectLinksDirectory/PreservationDigitalMaterial; The Australian PADI initiative hosts a huge range of information on digital preservation at http://www.nla.gov.au/padi/, particularly at http://www.nla.gov.au/padi/topics/44.html; Reference Model for an Open Archival Information System, http://ssdoo.gsfc.nasa.gov/nost/isoas/overview.html; and Gregory W. Lawrence, William R. Kehoe, Oya Y. Rieger, William H. Walters, and Anne R. Kenney, "Risk Management of Digital Information: A File Format Investigation (CLIR 2000)," http://www.clir.org/pubs/abstract/pub93abst.html.
8. Calimera, "Guidelines on Digitization," http://www.calimera.org/Lists/Guidelines/Digitization.htm#digitizationtitle.
9. Minerva Working Group 6, ed., *Good Practice Handbook*, 48
10. Electronic Resource Preservation and Access Network, http://www.erpanet.org/. The European Commission funded the ERPANET Project, which was established by a European consortium, to make available information pertaining to best practice and skills development in the area of digital preservation of cultural heritage and scientific objects.

11. *Standards*: ISO 8879:1986. Information Processing—Text and Office Systems—Standard Generalized Markup Language (SGML). Extensible Markup Language (XML) 1. 0, http://www.w3.org/TR/REC-xml/; Text Encoding Initiative (TEI), http://www.tei-c.org/; HTML 4.01 HyperText Markup Language, http://www.w3.org/TR/html401/; and XHTML 1.0 The Extensible HyperText Markup Language, http://www.w3.org/TR/xhtml1/.
Other references: Portable Document Format (PDF), http://www.adobe.com /products/acrobat/adobepdf.html.
Guidance: AHDS Guide to Good Practice, "Creating and Documenting Electronic Texts," http://ota.ahds.ac.uk/documents/creating/.
12. Raymond A. Lorie, "Long-Term Archiving of Digital Information" (IBM Research Report, May 2000).
13. Jeff Rothenberg, "Digital Information Lasts Forever—Or Five Years, Whichever Comes First," http://www.amibusiness.com/dps/rothenberg-arma.pdf# search='Jeff%20Rothenberg'.
14. Marilyn Deegan and Simon Tanner, "Digital Futures: Strategies for the Information Age" (London: Library Association Publishing, 2002). Minerva Europe, "Technical Guidelines for Digital Cultural Content Creation Programmes" (UKOLN, University of Bath, 2004), http://www.minervaeurope.org/structure /workinggroups/servprov/documents/techguid1_0.pdf. This document has been developed on behalf of the Minerva Project by UKOLN, University of Bath, in association with MLA and The Council for Museums, Libraries & Archives.

CHAPTER 8

Step 6: Running a Pilot for the Full Project

T he pilot phase of the project allows the project managers to test their analysis and theories in a practical environment on a small scale. This stage enables the manager to make appropriate corrections to the theories before scaling up and including all users and all data of the museum's holdings. This is the most important stage of the computerization project. It is in this stage that one becomes aware of the pitfalls or shortcomings of the envisioned project. Robert Baron, a museum computer consultant, reviews some of the major topics that need to be considered when beginning such a pilot.[1] This stage requires funding but in the long run will save money because many of the program's shortcomings can be corrected within the contractual requirements posed by the museum.

A pilot test takes all of the steps described in the earlier chapters and puts them into practice. Once the museum's characteristics have been defined, an appropriate database has been selected but not purchased, a needs analysis of the work flow of the museum has been completed, and the data meant for the database test have been compiled, then it is time to examine the theory on a small scale before full implementation. Many museums understand the importance of having curators—the end users—try out the database before purchasing it. Yet this is similar to a test drive preformed sitting in a parked car, as the curator cannot truly recreate his work flow in coordination with the database. For this reason, it is necessary to convert real museum data into the database on which tests will be performed so that a curator can assess (test drive) the program. The importance of real data in the database cannot be stressed enough as it adds multidimensionality to the program, which would otherwise have been schematic. The test has to be run for every level of museum user. For this reason, a representative of each level should be chosen to be part of the test drive.

To run this pilot requires a miniversion of the large-scale project. Hence, a skeleton of the eventual hardware, software, and staff must be in place to run the pilot. A table listing the museum's requirements and predicted costs for a pilot—the skeleton needs for hardware, software, and staff—can be found below.

TABLE 8.1   Estimated costs of pilot (staff, hardware, and software)

	Detailed Request	Cost in Dollars of Request
Human resources	Administrator, editor, translators, image person, typist	$50,000
Oracle licenses	Ten	$7,000
Foundations/networking	Conservation labs	$5,000
Computer hardware	2 + 1 upgrade	$25,000
Other hardware and software	Digital camera, memory, BN scanner, slide feeder, Cumulus cataloguing software	$20,000
Database conversions	Registration department	$20,000
Photographing, scanning, and typing	1,500 objects	$18,000
Office supplies	Office and phone	$5,000
Software maintenance	—	—
Collection management program	(Demo for free)	($300,000—full price)
Upgrades + memory	—	—
Total		$150,000

STAGES AND MILESTONES FOR A PILOT

The stages of the pilot reflect a smaller version of all the steps mentioned in the earlier chapters. An overview of the whole museum is important before beginning the pilot, but in essence during the pilot only a small number of users and their needs will be selected. This limits both the data converted and tested, and the interfacing and reports produced for the pilot, so only a limited budget and timetable are required. The steps below enumerate the stages of the pilot:

I. Needs and Requirements Analysis
  1. Analysis of work flow in museum
  2. Analysis of databases
  3. Analysis of fields for interfacing
  4. Analysis of users and authorizations
  5. Application to the database
II. Pilot Committee Meeting
III. Conversions
  1. Analysis of requirements
  2. Write programs for conversions
  3. Conversions
  4. Installation on loaned server
IV. Pilot Committee Meeting
V. Running the Pilot
  1. Tutorial for users
  2. Pilot Stage 1—testing in database company
  3. Reassessing Stage 1
  4. Pilot Stage 2—testing in the museum

VI. Summary of Pilot
    1. Conclusions of results
    2. Feedback from users
    3. Listing changes required
    4. Costs of changes priced by database company
VII. Decision to Purchase Database with Changes

For the pilot stage, end users should continue to update data in their current databases as the information in the demo database is only meant to test the program and not update the contents. Lessons learned on this pilot are taken into consideration for the final conversion and implementation stage. Only at this point will the real work begin within this database. To formulate these lessons, the database company should interview the users of the program in order to ascertain which changes should be made so that the program fits the museum's needs.

This wish list should be compiled as a collaborative effort between the database company and the collections database team. The database company should then respond to the list with an itemized cost of the total database plus improvements. This new proposal is then presented to the administrative steering committee which will analyze the changes that are listed and decide which changes will be performed based on budget constraints, the program's flexibility, and overall feasibility.

If the pilot is successful, having been applied to perhaps 1 percent to 10 percent of a large museum's collection with representative curators from each wing, then the program can be bought and the database can be implemented museum-wide.

TABLE 8.2 Timetable—days estimated for pilot

Stages and Milestones	Days
I. Needs Analysis	13
Analysis of work flow in Museum	2
Analysis of databases	8
Analysis of fields for interfacing	1
Analysis of users and authorizations	2
Application to database	2
II. Steering Committee Meeting	1
III. Conversions	28
Analysis of requirements	5
Write programs for conversions	15
Conversions	8
Installation on loaned server	3
IV. Steering Committee Meeting	1
Tutorial for users	2
Pilot Stage 1	12
Reassessing Stage 1	4
Pilot Stage 2	6
V. Summary of Project	1
Total Days of Pilot	114

THE ISRAEL MUSEUM, JERUSALEM PILOT

At the Israel Museum, Jerusalem (IMJ), there are three levels of users: curator, registrar, and public. There are fifty curators from three wings and a chief registrar. The public comprises not just the visitors at the gallery level, but also researchers who access storage areas and curators from other departments. In addition to the curatorial staff who inputs information on the status of an object, there are the curatorial service departments which include the restoration department, the shipping department, photo laboratories, and so on. These auxiliary departments also need access to information on objects and in some cases add additional information pertaining to the object.

The pilot was planned to test a small version of the entire museum and consisted of ten stations: six curators (two from each wing), the chief registrar, the restoration laboratory from within the curatorial department, the Internet department representing the public's needs, and the database team. The administration approved the costs, the curators for the stations were chosen, and a project committee was formed, comprising the collections database manager (the project manager), the computer systems manager, the chief registrar, the project manager from the database company, and the head of their company. A document was prepared by the museum summarizing the information that would be transferred to the database company.

The company then studied the information, expanded on it, and presented their queries to the museum project manager in order to prepare the framework for the pilot. This needs analysis was then mapped into the fields of the database. These fields were then filled with data from the museum using a conversion process, which pours information from older databases into the new database. The conversion process is very complicated and very expensive and should not be underestimated. QUALCAT (Quality Control in Cataloging) is the name given to a project at the University of Bradford that used an expert system to eliminate duplicate monographic cataloguing records.[2] First, records (in UK MARC format) are transferred into a relational database and the records are compared to determine whether there are duplicates (given the variation in record quality and cataloguing style, this is no trivial task); once duplicates are identified the system tests for record quality and identifies (based on defined criteria) the catalogue's best record for the title.

Multitiered levels of information and media were converted into the pilot program. A bilingual lexicon[3] of eighteen thousand terms, texts belonging to fifty thousand objects (10 percent of the museum's holdings) from information found in multiple older databases used by different levels of staff (registrar, curators, service department, Internet site, etc.) and some two thousand scanned images were linked during the conversion process (see Figure 8.1).

The pilot process was crucial (although expensive) as it helped the curators to relate to the database with real museum data in it and analyze its problems more accurately. The curators were trained to use the program. Over a period of a few days, they were given the opportunity to perform their usual tasks on the pilot version of the database.

FIGURE 8.1 Scheme for the multitiered information used in the conversion process of the pilot

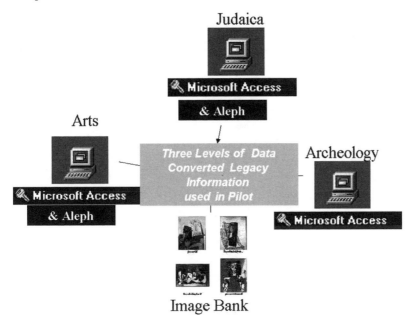

In the final stage of the pilot, conclusions from the testing stage were presented by each user and the project manager from the museum, and changes that could be accomplished with regard to either cost or practical computer application abilities were selected from the list. This list was then sent to the database company, which estimated the costs of these changes and adjustments for the database. The final price was then estimated, and the museum chose which changes would be incorporated into the final product.

The optimal end result will be the purchase of the database. The contract should include two very important clauses: the provision of long-term support and the promise that any future changes or developments the program might undergo, including those resulting from its use in other museums, would entitle the museum to an updated version.

NOTES

1. Robert Baron, "A Primer: Computerized Collection Management" *Registrar* 4, no. 2 (fall l987): 2–6.
2. For a description of one such conversion process, see F. H. Ayres, J. Cullen, C. Gierl, J. A. W. Huggill, M. J. Ridley, and I. S. Torsun, "QUALCAT: Automation of Quality Control in Cataloguing" (final report, British Library Research and Development Report, March 1991).
3. For more on the lexicon, see Allison Kupietzky, "Building a Bilingual Lexicon—A Case Study from the Israel Museum's Collection Database Project," in *Theme: US-Europe-Israel Cooperation In Culture X Technology*, ed. Violet Gilboa and James Hemsley (EVA 2002 Harvard Symposium Proceedings, Hampshire, UK: Vasari, 2002), chapter 7, 1–9.

CHAPTER 9

The Day after the Six-Step Process

After a successful pilot has been performed and a database program has been chosen as a collection management tool, the work begins in earnest. The day after completing the six-step process is the day the project is ready to begin assessing and carrying out development requests resulting from the pilot, contract signing, conversion and conversion checks, implementation, and training. The core group of end-users who participated in the pilot should meet to summarize their experiences and list all the program's faults with the intention of working with the database company to develop solutions to these problems. In most cases the list of changes to the program can be graded as Mandatory, Nice to Have, Not Applicable.[1] This list would then be sent to the database company in order for them to price the adjustments requested, taking into consideration the mandatory changes which, if not provided, would make the program not worth buying. A list of changes required might include development of unique fields for registration numbers, longer free text fields, the ability to print reports with pictures, a log for documenting changes in the program, and so forth.

At the end of this process the museum is ready to sign a contract that would include the price of the database, the price of the additional developments requested, the conversion costs of any legacy data, implementation, support, and tutorial costs. The museum's budget should include an additional 15 percent for hidden costs, such as additional hours performed by the database company for all the above work.

Upon signing the contract the entire museum should be included in a presentation in which the pilot process is presented and a timeline for the full project is explained. The socialization of this process is a very important stage and should include all future end-users. It is important to remember that until this stage those end-users were represented by the steering committee and the pilot users but were not part of the consensus. In order to receive a true consensus and assume acceptance of this tremendous change in work practice, all museum staff who will be using the database need to be included in the final stage of this process. This consensus should cover such issues as list of field names, the order of the fields, and the reports that will later be used by all.

A timeline should include milestone dates for the completion of the developments requested, the conversion process, implementation, and tutorial lessons. In addition, up to six months may be needed to check the converted information and to correct any mistakes, including deleting duplicate catalogue cards that may have been generated from multiple sources. A successful museum database project as explained earlier (see chapter 5 regarding staffing), should have a help desk staff that is capable of training and supporting the users on a daily basis. This help desk serves as a liaison with the computer company for future development changes or conversion requests. On average it could take about five hours to train new users. Once a new user begins to work in the database applying the new work flow, there is an adjustment period often resulting in a reconsideration or change to the work flow. An increased request for hardware, that is, computers, scanners, server space, and staff, may be the result of a successfully implemented project. Some museums make use of volunteers and interns during this time since there is so much information to handle, but their skills are basic, and therefore the curator should be involved to verify the quality of data input or changes. On average the curator needs to spend almost half an hour reviewing each catalogue card. Although this is a large amount of time if one needs to review two thousand works of art, some curators might use this opportunity to physically revisit each object, for example, remeasure, look at its condition. While this will slow down the process even more, it will aid in achieving a very high level of cataloguing. Entering information is the first aspect to digitizing the collection, but once many people begin using the program, the other aspect of search retrieval and reports becomes the more important task. Therefore, once installed it is necessary to spend time fine-tuning the search capabilities and creating report templates that can answer multiple needs. If the museum is independent of the database company for these changes, then the cost and technical issues will not be prohibitive, and in the long run the users will be much happier.

In addition to the retroactive work they will have as a result of the conversion process, the museum staff needs to accept that from that day on each of its new objects will be entered correctly into the database. Changing work habits for all the staff members involved is a very time-consuming process, but it is ultimately worthwhile. If all staff members are involved from the very beginning in the decision-making process, there will be less resistance to the implementation of the project. This period will test the success or failure of the socialization process within the museum.

NOTE

1. Grading terminology from The Canadian Heritage Information Network (CHIN) published a different test on their Web site. See "Collections Management Software Review—Criteria Checklist," http://www.chin.gc.ca /English/Collections_Management/Software_Selection/English/Doc/criteria _checklist.doc.

CHAPTER **10**

Publication and Copyrights

A lthough this book is focused on digitization of collections for museum staff, a few words on copyright and information access must be added. Once the SAGE-K process is completed, a database purchased and implemented, and the collections digitized, the museum is ready to allow public access to the collections. Five topics need to be considered:

- Reason for sharing information with the public
- What should be shared with the public
- How to share information—in what format
- Costs of sharing and storing information
- How to present packaged information to the public

REASON FOR SHARING INFORMATION WITH THE PUBLIC

Museums, libraries, and archives hold and create digital or multimedia content, which may include newspapers, photographs, maps, manuscripts, sound recordings, local art collections, and film or video. These repositories have an obligation on their part to disclose this information to the greater public. It is documented in the International Council of Museums (ICOM) Code of Ethics for Museums, 2006, that a basic mission of museums is to "hold primary evidence for establishing and furthering knowledge." In paragraph 3.2, it states

Availability of Collections
Museums have a particular responsibility for making collections and all relevant information available as freely as possible, having regard to restraints arising for reasons of confidentiality and security.

(See Appendix IV—International Council of Museums (ICOM), "Statutes," Code of Professional Ethics.)[1]
This leads to the question, what should be shared with the public?

WHAT SHOULD BE SHARED WITH THE PUBLIC

Research and publication opportunities need to be restricted in coordination with the confidentiality act and copyright issues set out in the ICOM Code of Ethics for Museums, 2006. A good rule of thumb is anything that appears in the public domain should be the first items considered for publication. This includes objects published in catalogues, displayed in an exhibition, or in the permanent collection of the museum. In most museums this can be anywhere from 10 percent to 20 percent of the collection. The quality and the quantity of information to be shared with the public is a decision the museums' staff needs to grapple with from the start.

HOW TO SHARE INFORMATION—IN WHAT FORMAT

While the computerization of collections is focused on the needs of the museums' staff, the resulting digital information is a treasure trove of shared cultural heritage for the public. The balance between printed material, multimedia holdings, and Internet resources has changed rapidly over the last few years in heritage institutions, and it is now accepted that all these formats have a role to play in providing and managing "virtual" as well as physical resources. The ICOM Code of Ethics for Museums, 2006, has a section entitled "Museums provide opportunities for the appreciation, understanding and promotion of the natural and cultural heritage." In paragraph 4.1, it states

> *Displays, Exhibitions and Special Activities*
> Displays and temporary exhibitions, physical or *electronic*, should be in accordance with the stated mission, policy and purpose of the museum. They should not compromise either the quality or the proper care and conservation of the collections.[2]

This idea clearly brings into focus the realization that museums are now displaying and publishing information in electronic or digital media. The innovative interfacing of virtual objects and online educational activities acts as an electronic surrogate and extends the museums' holdings beyond the walls of the museum experience.[3]

There are a variety of publication formats and delivery methods. Once the data have reached a satisfactory level of digitization in the database as described in the SAGE-K method, the options for exporting the information to a user-friendly interface are virtually unlimited. The digital material created by and for curators to meet their daily needs does not answer the public's needs in the same way. A database interfacing is created with ease of data entry in mind. The search facilities are also for research purposes and therefore not necessarily easy for the average visitor to use. The museum's visitor would prefer an interface that allows the visitor to peruse the collection at a glance, visually associating topics and items while moving along rapidly from one item to the next. The visitor's different access methods and search needs require a more user-friendly tool to access the collection. In addition the data found in the database are not meant for public consumption, and often there are research questions posed in the texts. This means that the information needs to be edited for the public. The curatorial database information therefore serves only as a springboard for the public information database. Once exported from the curatorial database, the information needs to be both edited and inserted into a new environment for public access.

The Getty ArtAccess stations found on the museum's grounds use a delivery interfacing, different from that of the curatorial database, which serves as a good example of a working export mechanism. Some one hundred items a week are exported from the curators' database into a buffer area where a team of editors of texts and images works to refine the information, which is then placed into the ArtAccess search mechanism built for the public.[4] Information that is retrieved from the curator's database can be presented in two formats: static (disconnected from the source database) and dynamic (linked to the source database).

In a static environment there is more control of the visual manipulation of the material. Programs such as Flash and Director by Macromedia are the primary choices for this medium in a museum setting because it is possible to reach highly painterly screens. This often requires the help of a talented graphic designer. Searches are usually not truly textual searches but rather preconceived routes of information, sometimes referred to as virtual tours, where one button leads you to the next.

In a dynamic environment the material does not lose its connection with the database. The method of presentation is usually quite linear, and not experiential, although this is changing as Macromedia is working toward this end. In most cases a PHP or ASP file is used to connect between the fields and the delivery screens.[5] The ability for the information to stay "live" or dynamic is a plus as changes to the textual or visual material occurs on the fly. Search mechanisms are easier to apply to a textual field-based data structure, which permits greater flexibility and more complex search options.

STANDARDS

Standards for the digitization of information for the public differ in quality from those used in the museum's cataloguing process. Unlike archival standards that are discussed earlier (see Images—Quality and Storage heading in chapter 7), it is a good idea to reduce the size of the images for public consumption. This is both for ease of accessibility, as lower resolution images download faster, and because of copyright issues. Digitized images should be uploaded onto the Internet in JPEG format. It is worth considering providing images in various resolutions. This allows for readability appropriate to the context of use.

IPR (Intellectual Property Rights) issues may also contribute to decisions about the size and quality of images provided (72 dpi 100 × 100 pixels for thumbnails and 400 × 400 pixels for large images are found in many museums; see Appendix VIII—Fifteen Worldwide Museum Sites Reviewed). It is advisable to consider using the museum's information centers as the preferred setting for showing larger audio and video files. There is a possibility that the users' access to video may be constrained by bandwidth restrictions, and it may be necessary to provide a range of files or streams of different quality.

The key to successful searching using a dynamic structure is in essence the preplanning associated with metadata standards. (See the following: section headings: Can a Common Platform Be Achieved for the Museum World? in chapter 1, Texts—Quality and Storage in chapter 7, File Formats in chapter 7.)

The use of appropriate metadata is very important for enabling search and retrieval of material from digital collections. This is even more important when searching across multiple collections stored in different locations. Many metadata models already exist. Therefore each institution has to choose a metadata model suited to its own goals. It is advisable to avoid creating a new one, unless the requirements of the project are seriously underserved by all existing standards. Time spent modeling the important characteristics of the material being digitized and identifying its key attributes and descriptors will be time well invested. Such a model can then be compared with the scope and features of existing metadata models. Possible controlled vocabularies (e.g., to describe a location or an artist) should be identified. Several such vocabularies already exist and can greatly increase the success of searches, and so on. (For more on lexicons, see section titled Lexicon in chapter 7.)

COSTS OF SHARING AND STORING INFORMATION

Once the decision to share the digital collection with the public has been made, the financial implications need to be considered. The move toward digital content is also having an impact on space allocation, as users require computers and other equipment in order to be able to make use of digital resources on the premises. In the section titled Budgeting for the Project in Chapter 5, it was noted that the time and costs of digitizing an object for internal use would be around one hour and $10. However, in order to reach a level of digitization suitable for the public the time and costs need to be doubled. This is because the object's information needs to be edited, both the textual data and the visual data. If the museum is required to publish all information in two or more languages, a minimum of another hour needs to be added to the total time it takes to digitize. Thus a figure of $30 is the estimated cost for a bilingual catalogued object suitable for the public. Staff will require additional training, and new resource management models will need to be developed. This is expensive, but it also enables the implementation of one of the most basic missions of museums: to share information with the public. The type of object and its condition will also have an effect on the length of time it will take to digitize. Objects, such as glass slides and old manuscripts, which are more fragile, will need to be handled with greater patience and care. The storage space required for the public access projects needs to be considered when budgeting for such projects. Because the images need to be duplicated from the curatorial database and relinked to the new

FIGURE 10.1 An example of a high-resolution image from the Library of Congress image server freely available to the public online (The Library of Congress generally does not own rights to material in its collections and cannot grant or deny permission to publish or distribute material in its collections.)

Jerusalem from the Mount of Olives, published 1842
David Roberts, R.A., England, 1796–1864, artist
Louis Haghe, 1806–1885, lithographer
Color lithograph
Library of Congress Collection, LC-USZC4-3429

database material formulated for public access, the images, video, and audio files need to have a server dedicated to this project. The server costs were reviewed earlier. (See also Multimedia—Quality and Storage and Long-Term Storage Solutions in chapter 7.)

HARDWARE AND SOFTWARE

Variations exist in the types of hardware and software employed by users. The delivery of effective multimedia services requires bandwidth. The levels of bandwidth restriction within which users operate affect the speed and availability of downloading large files. It is therefore critical for those creating digital media to consider the average household's bandwidth and regard this bandwidth as the lowest common denominator. This bandwidth should be tested with large files to see how long, on average, the downloading time is when considering sharing large files. To maximize the potential, audience resources should be available in alternative sizes or formats or at alternative resolutions/bit rates.

REUSE AND REPURPOSING

Heritage institutions will want to repackage and repurpose material that has been developed by their costly digitization projects. In order to facilitate this reuse, the implementation of standards will be important. Because of the variety of formats available, standards are needed to ensure interoperability and to combat obsolescence. (See the guidelines on digitization, digital preservation guidelines, and long-term storage solutions in chapter 7.) In order to facilitate potential exchange and interoperability between services, it is suggested that projects be able to provide item level descriptions in the form of simple, unqualified Dublin Core Metadata records and provide item-level descriptions conforming to the DC.Culture schema (see Appendix I—Field Names and Standards: The Dublin Core Element Set).[6] Accessibility for special populations, such as the disabled, is also very important and should be included in the planning for making the museum's collections accessible online to all the institution's constituents.

ACCESSIBILITY

The availability of audiovisual materials and their associated equipment can be useful for young children, people with low levels of literacy, and those who use another language and might find oral and visual communication easier than the printed word.

The assurance of accessibility for all users, including disabled people, to multimedia resources is of key importance. (See the Calimera guidelines on accessibility for disabled people, http://www.calimera.org/Lists/Guidelines /Accessibility_for_disabled_people.htm#accessibilitytitle).

People who are handicapped can be assisted by the world of computers, for example, large print, automated reading for the blind, and so on. (For an interesting analysis of accessibility in United Kingdom Web sites, see "Quality of UK Cultural Websites: Evaluation" by Kate Fernie, at http://www .minervaeurope.org/events/fernie050407.ppt.)

Projects need to be accessible by a variety of browsers, hardware systems, automated programs, and end-users. Web sites need to be accessible by a wide range of browsers and hardware devices (e.g., personal digital assistants [PDAs] as well as PCs). Web sites should also be accessible by browsers that support W3C recommendations such as HTML/XHTML, Cascading Style Sheets (CSS), and the Document Object Model (DOM). The World Wide Web Consortium (W3C) develops technologies (specifications, guidelines, software, and tools) to help the Internet achieve its full potential. Projects that include proprietary file formats, for example, Microsoft Word, Excel, and PowerPoint documents, and browser plug-in technologies, need to ensure that their content is still accessible by browsers that do not have the proprietary software or plug-ins.

LEARNING RESOURCE CREATION

It is important when planning projects to consider the potential reuse of the resources created and to recognize that end-users or third parties may wish to extract elements of a given resource and repackage them with parts of other resources from their own collections and from other sources. An area in which this can play a large role is the educational sector. Projects that develop learning resources should be aware of the IEEE Learning Object Metadata (LOM) standard and should consider providing LOM descriptions of their learning resources.[7]

PRESENTATION OF PACKAGED INFORMATION FOR THE PUBLIC

Collections of virtual resources can be created from curatorial database information. These presentation methods are a way of extending conventional museum services. There are many presentation methods available today. All methods need to take into account that access should not be limited to the general public but to all visitors, whether handicapped or disabled.

The content, once created or harvested from past projects, needs to be wrapped or packaged for public consumption. Digitization and the Internet have revolutionized the delivery of multimedia content. Newly emerging technologies now offer museums, libraries, and archives opportunities to extend and improve services and to reach wider population groups. There are a number of possibilities available but none as far reaching as the Internet, accessible from a home computer. The options are not mutually exclusive— choosing one method does not mean that you cannot use other methods for packaging simultaneously. On the contrary, it is highly recommended to reuse costly digital material.

Connection with the public via kiosks in the galleries, sit-down stations in information centers, PDA, or audio guides are all methods of delivery. There are a number of delivery options and hardware solutions that can be used in presenting the information to the public. In most cases, each method attracts different users.

The range of devices, or delivery channels, which can be used to access multimedia services is increasing, and includes Third-Generation Technology (3G) mobile phones, PDAs, kiosks, digital and interactive TV, and digital media players.[8] Small, often portable devices can now deliver information and integrate personal services in an electronic format.

Many methods of presentation exist. Below is a review a few of these methods, namely, E-books, 3D and Virtual Reality, Visualization, Haptics, Kiosks, Video Conferencing, Mobile Services, Tour Guides, Geographic Information Systems (GIS), and the Internet. A partial list of guidelines is available on Calimera's Web site at http://www.calimera.org/Lists/Guidelines/multimediascope.

E-BOOKS

E-books and e-serials are a way of packaging text electronically. An e-book is a text or monograph that is available in an electronic form. It can be downloaded from the Internet and can be read on a variety of hardware platforms such as a computer or a handheld device.

3D AND VIRTUAL REALITY (VR)

VR is the simulation of a real or imagined environment that can be experienced visually in three dimensions. It differs from other three-dimensional graphics media in that it is interactive, enabling the user to move around within the space, for example, to tour a virtual exhibition. Three-dimensional virtual reality "fly through" models are used, for example, in the reconstruction of vanished or ruined monuments or in simulating whole areas of an ancient landscape.[9] Many 3D projects have been successfully completed in European Heritage Institutions. For a list of some examples of projects accomplished by EPOCH, see http://www.epoch-net.org/.[10]

The guidelines for digital renderings of 3D and virtual reality material are tied to the "Catch-22" of finding a balance between quality and file size on the Internet and providing an easily available player for the finished product. Projects that make use of three-dimensional virtual reality "fly throughs" and models should consider the needs of users accessing their site using typical computers and modem connections. When projects are being planned, the usability of the models should be considered, and they should be tested using typical modem connections and home, school, or library computer systems with a variety of typical operating systems and browsers. Viewers for 3D and virtual reality material are not yet widely distributed with operating system software. This contrasts with image, audio, and video, which are commonly provided with Windows software that ensures that viewers for any 3D or virtual reality material are readily available. Standards in this area continue to evolve, but virtual reality models need to be compatible with the X3D specification. Apple's QuickTime virtual reality (QTVR) is not a true 3D image format, but does offer useful functionality. Projects that do not require the full functionality of X3D might consider using QTVR instead.[11]

VISUALIZATION

Visualization is the term used to describe the use of computer graphics to present and analyze information. Two-dimensional (2D) visualization includes charts and graphs, for example, pie charts, histograms, line-graphs, contour plots, and scatter plots. Three-dimensional (3D) visualization uses techniques such as ISO-surfaces, 3D vector plots, volume rendering techniques, and so forth or a combination of these. The use of animation adds movement to 3D visualization. For example, "flybys" allow the viewer to see all sides of a static object (e.g., a vase), and "motion observation" allows the viewer to watch the object itself move (e.g., a machine in action). Visualization techniques have all sorts of potential applications. For example they can be used to create visual reconstructions of people or objects from excavated remains, or to see what effect a volcano erupting would have on a landscape.

HAPTICS

Haptics enable users to "touch" and "feel" objects via a computer by using special input/output devices (e.g., data gloves). This adds another dimension to the experience of virtual reality and can be useful for visually disabled people.[12] For a discussion of haptics, see DigiCULT Technology Watch Briefing no. 13: Telepresence, Haptics, Robotics, April 2004.

KIOSKS

Public access online and Internet kiosks need to be strategically placed where people who have free time and are looking for information can easily access them. They also should be multifunctional. Within a building a well-designed kiosk can deal with a number of routine tasks such as membership applications, frequently asked questions, directions to areas of the building, book requests, ticket purchases, as well as provide access to the Internet. Important decisions in kiosk design include whether the data are loaded locally on a PC at each kiosk or updated remotely, whether the kiosk is offline or connected to a network and/or the Internet, whether it has telephone access to a help desk, and handling methods of antivandalism security. Kiosks can also include the ability to print.

VIDEO CONFERENCING

Video conferencing allows for two or more people in different places to see and hear each other, and sometimes to share work on their own computers. Multisite video conferencing is possible, linking many sites together at one time.

Video conferencing takes place over telephone networks so high bandwidth is required. The basic ingredients for a video conference system are transmitting and receiving equipment at each site and an intervening network to carry the signals. Input devices could be microphones, television cameras, white boards, and so forth, and output devices could be loudspeakers, television picture monitors, data screens, white boards, and so forth. For video conferencing to become really successful interoperability of equipment is essential.[13]

MOBILE SERVICES

Mobile handheld devices are becoming increasingly small and multifunctional. Mobile phones can now act as telephones, calculators, personal organizers, calendars, cameras, Internet servers, e-mail senders and receivers, e-book readers, enable users to play games, and so on. PDAs can play music and show video films.

The delivery of digital multimedia content to handheld devices is already possible. Therefore anything that can be accessed via the Internet will be accessible on a PDA. Ways in which cultural heritage institutions can utilize mobile technology might include promoting services, advertising exhibitions and events, sending personalized messages such as information about events of interest to a particular individual, reminders of overdue books or reservations ready to be collected, and answering enquiries. Useful advice on developing content for mobile devices can be found on the Canadian Heritage

Information Network Web site. However, using the positioning potential of mobile access via wireless communication technology, cultural institutions can also offer services such as personalized tour guides.

TOUR GUIDES

Audio guides are now very common in museums and heritage sites to guide people around an exhibition or outdoor attraction, but can also be used in museums, libraries, and archives as an alternative to printed guides to explain systems or services. They are often available in more than one language.

Audio guides are increasingly being replaced by handheld wireless devices, which are much more flexible. They can, for example, be personalized to a group or individual, and can contain interactive features. In addition to audio, images, text, graphics, and video can be delivered to the PDA. Content can be stored on a central computer server and relayed to visitors via a wireless local area network (WLAN) when and where they need it. Visitors can borrow PDAs or use their own, downloading maps or floor plans and other information at the start of the visit. This technology offers a number of advantages, including accessibility (it can be tailored to the special needs of visitors); flexibility (it enables users to make their own way around and access information in greater or lesser detail as they wish); convenience (it can be easier to read or listen to information from a handheld device than from a printed label or guidebook); and personalization (information can be delivered in different languages or aimed at different audiences, e.g., children or experts).

GEOGRAPHIC INFORMATION SYSTEMS

Much cultural content has grounding in a geographic place, for example, the object's country of origin, the book's publisher, and so on. This "grounding" of the cultural heritage items offers a powerful means by which content might be grouped or retrieved. Geographic information systems (GIS) are software applications specifically designed to store, manipulate, and retrieve place-based information, and they are increasingly widely deployed within the cultural heritage sector. It is not necessary, however, for every project that wishes to store place-based information, or to include a location map on their Web site, to install and maintain a GIS. Place-based information may be stored within a traditional database, and simple images of location maps and so on may be created by various means. It is wise to ensure that a project can support a GIS implementation in the future, even if this is not initially planned within the project.[14]

THE INTERNET

It is expected that end-user access to resources will be primarily through the use of Internet protocols. Preparation for publication requires the processing of the "digital master" to generate digital objects suitable for use in the

Internet context, typically by reducing quality in order to generate files of sizes suitable for transfer over networks.

In addition, video and audio material may be made available either for download or for streaming, which means that instead of the entire file being transferred, a small buffer space is created on the user's computer, and data are transmitted into the buffer. As soon as the buffer is full, the streaming file starts to play, while more data continue to be transmitted. When preparing information for a web delivery format, reducing the required material to the most common denominator is a key to broad public accessibility. For this reason lower resolution images and multimedia that is streamed is recommended. Internet penetration continues to grow rapidly and cultural heritage sites need to adjust to the new realities. Surveys fielded in 2006 show that Internet penetration among adults in the United States has hit an all-time high. A survey from April 2006 shows that fully 73 percent of respondents (about 147 million adults) are Internet users, up from 66 percent (about 133 million adults) in our January 2005 survey. The share of Americans who have broadband connections at home has now reached 42 percent (about 84 million), up from 29 percent (about 59 million) in January 2005.[15]

Streaming media should be considered by heritage sites so as to share large files with the general public. Streaming media is a sequence of moving images and/or sounds sent in compressed form usually over the Internet. Some of the programs used to stream media require frequent updating, and some, particularly those used to download audio and video, are bandwidth heavy and may involve long download times. Streaming media enables people to view films, listen to music, and handle other large files in a shorter amount of time. It does this by partly downloading the entire file of a multimedia object, for example, a film, as it allows the information to be viewed in a streaming method. With the use of streaming media, the user does not have to wait to download a large file before seeing the video or hearing the sound. Instead, the media is sent in a continuous stream and is played as it arrives. For guidelines on this method, see http://www.calimera.org/Lists/Guidelines /multimediascope. Streaming media software examples include RealAudio and MS Media Server. A number of other streaming media programs exist.

Many digitization projects in the cultural area lead to the creation of online cultural resources, usually a Web site with images, metadata, 3D artifacts, and so on. They range from the simplest content sites to complex, software-driven portals and viewing engines. A large body of knowledge exists on the creation of Web sites; only a few guidelines are provided here.[16] Web sites should be easy to navigate; it is important that links to the front page or to a table of contents are easily accessible and in working order. Sufficient attention should be paid to universal access and to the utilization of Web sites by the partially sighted and other disabled persons. It is recommended that web pages be short enough to minimize the amount of scrolling necessary by the user. Images should be small enough not to disrupt the browsing experience. Larger images can be given a link from the Web pages, with a note to the effect that the image is large and downloading may be slow. The use of animations, pop-ups, pop-unders, Flash, and similar technologies should be utilized with care. It is best to avoid lengthy introductory animation sequences. Web sites should ideally be multilingual, with at least the host country language and one or two other languages supported. Links to external resources need to be verified on a periodic basis, in order to minimize dead links.

COPYRIGHTS

A copyright is the exclusive right of authors with regard to the use of their original works. It exists from the moment of *fixation* in a tangible medium of expression (including software). It includes the right of the author to control the reproduction, copying, display, performance, and other uses of a work.

The publication of any material online must be accompanied by some consideration of the Intellectual Property Rights (IPR) associated with the material.[17] For material that is in the public domain (such as particularly old books or newspapers or material placed explicitly in the public domain), there is relatively little difficulty with regard to copyrights. However, many cultural institutions derive revenue from the use of images of artifacts or images in their collections and so are very defensive of their copyrighted material. In addition, material with copyrights held by third parties can only be published with the consent of such third parties. A range of technical options is available to protect the copyright of material placed on the Internet.

The initial step when exploring the copyright situation for a cultural item is to establish the ownership of that copyright. The legal situation should be established with regard to copyright and publication in the country where the project is being carried out. Each country has its own copyright laws. Such laws usually apply to all forms of publication, including online publication. They may, or may not, cover the act of digitization, which may be construed to be an archiving process, or may be considered copying. On no account should online publication go ahead without a copyright being sought. Certain items, for example, old newspapers, have clear copyright rules governing them. Typically these allow free copying once the papers are of a certain age. Items that fit into this category can be freely digitized and published. For items whose copyright is vested in the institution carrying out the project, internal permission will be required for digitization and online publication. For items whose copyright is held by a third party, such as the lender or donor of a collection of historical items, that party's permission must be sought, in writing. Only when such permission has been received, can publication go ahead. Securing permission to digitize and publish may involve payment. The amount of payment must be balanced against the value of including the relevant item(s) in the online resource.[18]

The publication of items online is an open invitation to make copies of the items. It is impossible to prevent some level of copying of material displayed on the Web. However, there are a number of possible procedures that can be considered, each of which has some effect in the safeguarding of copyright. The approach that is most appropriate for any one project will depend to a large degree on the goals of the project and the cultural institution, as well as on the nature of the material. In general, the publication of a small selection of images, at low resolution, is a common approach for online galleries and museums. (See common resolutions used by museums' Web sites reviewed in Appendix VIII—Fifteen Worldwide Museum Sites Reviewed.) The relative uniqueness of many cultural holdings provides proof of ownership of copyright in many situations.[19]

It should be established whether copyright needs are to be safeguarded. Procedures that are used to safeguard a copyright should be agreed on with the copyright holders. The following procedures are among those that could be considered: protection mechanisms and encryption of images.

Protection mechanisms, for example, encryption and watermarking, add a visible or invisible watermark or copyright stamp to each image. Such marks can be used to prove the ownership of a "stolen" image, as well as to track the use of the image across the Internet.

Encryption of images involves issuing an appropriate key only to registered users. This, of course, reduces the value of the online image to the rest of the public while restricting publication to low-resolution images, such as 75 dpi for screen viewing. This also restricts the degree to which images can be used in other domains, such as online or printing. Often this method is used to restrict publication to only small parts of an image. The Italian DADDI project (see http://www.xlimage.it/italiacina2006/index.php?lang=ENG) is an example of a project using this method. The project displays images only to registered, authorized members of a particular community.

NOTES

1. Version quoted is correct for 2005. From 2006, there is an updated version, which can be found at http://icom.museum/ethics.html#intro.
2. Ibid.
3. Susan Hazan, "The Israel Museum and the Electronic Surrogate," Cultivate Interactive, October 2001, http://www.cultivate-int.org/issue5/israel/#ref-02.
4. The author visited the Getty Center and interviewed the editing team of ArtAccess in August 1999. Special thanks goes to Ken Hamma who set up the behind-the-scenes tour.
5. PHP is a script language and interpreter that is freely available and used primarily on Linux Web servers. PHP, originally derived from Personal Home Page Tools, now stands for PHP: Hypertext Preprocessor, which is an alternative to Microsoft's Active Server Page (ASP) technology. As with ASP, the PHP script is embedded within a Web page along with its HTML. Before the page is sent to a user that has requested it, the Web server calls PHP to interpret and perform the operations called for in the PHP script. An HTML page that includes a PHP script is typically given a file name suffix of ".php," ".php3," or ".phtml." Like ASP, PHP can be thought of as "dynamic HTML pages," since content will vary based on the results of interpreting the script. PHP is free and offered under an open source license. SearchOpenSource.com Definitions.

6. Dublin Core Metadata Initiative, "Dublin Core Metadata Element Set, version 1.1," http://dublincore.org/documents/dces/; Minerva Europe, "DC. Culture," http://www.minervaeurope.org/DC.Culture.htm.

7. *Standards*: IEEE Learning Object Metadata, http://ltsc.ieee.org/wg12/; IMS Global Learning Consortium, Inc., http://www.imsproject.org/; and IMS Content Packaging, http://www.imsproject.org/content/packaging/.
   Sources: Minerva Europe, "Technical Guidelines for Digital Cultural Content Creation Programmes" (UKOLN, University of Bath, 2004), http://www .minervaeurope.org/structure/workinggroups/servprov/documents/techguid1_0. pdf. This document has been developed on behalf of the Minerva Project by UKOLN, University of Bath, in association with MLA, The Council for Museums, Libraries & Archives.

8. The EU IST program explicitly supports movement toward the future generation of technologies in which computers and networks will be integrated into the everyday environment, and defines multimedia as "Using computers and/ or digital features to present visual and audio content in a meaningful context. Elements include: animation, audio components, CD-ROM, computer entertainment, convergence media, data compression, DVD, graphics and graphics interfaces, hypermedia, text, video, videoconferencing, virtual reality, ... and an ever expanding list of technologies in this growth area" (http://www.calimera .org/Lists/Guidelines/#multimediaref1).

9. See Calimera Guideline, "Interactivity," http://www.calimera.org/Lists /Guidelines/Interactivity.htm#interactivityvirtualreality.

10. EPOCH Web site, http://www.epoch-net.org/.

11. *Standards*: Web3D Consortium, http://www.web3d.org/; X3D, http://www .web3d.org/x3d.html; and QuickTime VR, http://www.apple.com/quicktime /qtvr/.
    Guidance: Archaeology Data Service VR Guide to Good Practice, http:// ads.ahds.ac.uk/project/goodguides/g2gp.html.

12. See Calimera Guidelines, "Accessibility for Disabled People," http:// www.calimera.org/Lists/Guidelines/Accessibility_for_disabled_people.htm #accessibilitytitle. Also see an interesting analysis of accessibility in United Kingdom Web sites, by Kate Fernie, "Quality of UK Cultural Websites: Evaluation," http://www.minervaeurope.org/events/fernie050407.ppt.

13. The main standards are H.320 and H.323. See http://www.calimera.org/Lists /Guidelines/#multimediaref34.

14. *Standards*: OpenGIS Consortium, http://www.opengis.org/.
    Guidance: Archaeology Data Service GIS Guide to Good Practice, http:// ads.ahds.ac.uk/project/goodguides/gis/.

15. Pew Internet & American Life Project, "Internet Penetration and Impact," 2006, http://www.pewinternet.org/PPF/r/182/report_display.asp.

16. For a full list of Web site criteria, see Minerva Working Group 5, ed., "Quality Principles for Cultural Websites: A Handbook," http://www.minervaeurope .org/publications/qualitycommentary/qualitycommentary050314final.pdf.

17. Maxine K. Sitts, ed., *Handbook for Digital Projects: A Management Tool for Preservation and Access*, 1st ed. (Andover, Massachusetts: Northeast Document Conservation Center, 2000); Melissa Smith Levine, "Overview of Legal Issues for Digitization," in *Handbook for Digital Projects: A Management Tool for Preservation and Access*, ed. Maxine K. Sitts (Andover, Massachusetts: Northeast

Document Conservation Center, 20000, http://www.nedcc.org/digital /v.htm#copyright.

Sources: Interoperability and Service Provision, European Working Group Intellectual Property Right; Subgroup, http://www.minervaeurope.org /structure/workinggroups/servprov/ipr/documents/wp4ipr040806.pdf; Arts and Humanities Data Service (AHDS), http://ahds.ac.uk/copyrightfaq.htm; U.S. Copyright Office, http://www.copyright.gov/circs/circ1.html; and Museum Computer Network, http://www.mcn.edu/groups/index.asp?subkey=100.

18. For a concise list of rules governing visual material, see UK: MCG Copyright in Museums and Galleries, http://www.mda.org.uk/mcopyg/index.htm.

19. TASI, "Copyright and Digital Images," http://www.tasi.ac.uk/advice/managing /copyright.html; PADI, "Copyright," http://www.nla.gov.au/padi/topics /392.html; IFLA copyright page, http://www.ifla.org/II/cpyright.htm; Digimarc digital watermarks, www.digimarc.com; Signumtech digital watermarks, www.signumtech.com; audio digital watermarks, www.musicode.com; watermarking overview, http://www.webreference.com/content/watermarks/; general United Kingdom copyright information, http://www.copyrightservice.co.uk /copyright/protecting(02).htm; and AHDS, "Copyright FAQ," http://ahds.ac.uk /copyrightfaq.htm.

CHAPTER 11

Conclusion

Not so long ago museums began to deal with a global issue: how best to incorporate increasingly necessary computer-based organization and management tools into their existing museum structure. Merging the museum and computer worlds is a challenge for any museum—even more so for a multilingual museum, because of the difficulty of providing tools capable of input and access in more than one language, particularly Semitic languages that are read in different directions, right to left and left to right.

The discovery process for the best way to go about digitizing a museum collection in a multilingual environment is a long one. It requires research into what other museums have done, an in-depth analysis of the needs of specific museums, and a survey of available database products and service providers. In addition, the socialization process in the museum needs to be planned and dissemination of information to appropriate museum staff and administration examined so that all levels of staff are involved in the decision-making process. These essential stages, necessary for the planning of the project budget and funding, require institutional approval in the early stages so that in the later stages, implementation and training can progress smoothly.

The first section of this book presented a comprehensive study of museums and their computer systems (including databases, lexicons, and implementation needs), what is available, what is used worldwide, pitfalls, and successes. Following this review was an analysis of the process through which a mono- or multilingual museum must proceed in order to achieve computerization of its collections—the SAGE-K (Six-step Activation Guideline for E-Kulture) process. This methodology can be applied to museums and cultural institutions worldwide. The examination of the computer process in the museum ends with instructions for carrying out the pilot, which tests the planned database program. The pilot is followed by a complete implementation of the database within the museum, at first with its staff and later with its public constituents.

In this complex process there are two critical elements essential to making the computerization of multilingual collections a success: the collections database manager and the implementation process which should include the use of a multilingual lexicon. The collections database manager should be an on-staff member who oversees the entire project. This manager should have working knowledge of both museology and computer science. Having one staff member skilled in both fields allows for a thorough coordination on all levels of the project. By constructing or applying a multilingual lexicon within the computer database program, terminology is both unified and translated. By establishing a set of terms that are synonymous, and being thorough enough to include variations and flexible enough to add new lexicon terms as necessary, the museum can create a database that can serve the multilingual needs of both its staff and its constituents. Finally, by developing an efficient and accurate process to implement a database in the museum setting, the museum enables information regarding the history of its art objects to be made accessible to both its staff and its global constituents for research, edification, and enjoyment.

Field Names and Standards: The Dublin Core Element Set

The Dublin Core itself consists of thirteen core elements, each of which may be further extended by the use of SCHEME and TYPE qualifiers.

TABLE I.1 The Dublin Core

Element Name	Element Description
Subject	The topic addressed by the object being described
Title	The name of the object
Author	The person(s) primarily responsible for the intellectual content of the object
Publisher	The agent or agency responsible for making the object available
Other Agent	The person(s), such as editors and transcribers, who have made other significant intellectual contributions to the work
Date	The date of publication
Object Type	The genre of the object, such as novel, poem, or dictionary
Form	The data format of the object, such as Postscript, HTML, etc.
Identifier	String or number used to uniquely identify the object
Relation	Relationship between this and other objects
Source	Objects, either print or electronic, from which this object is derived
Language	Language of the intellectual content
Coverage	The spatial locations and temporal duration characteristic of the object

Source: From Paul Miller. Metadata for the masses. http://www.ariadne.ac.uk/issue5/metadata-masses/#core.

International and National Standards Initiatives

The museum and cultural heritage information standards and organizations listed below was originally compiled by the Getty Information Institute (formerly the Getty Art History Information Program, now incorporated in the Getty Research Institute) and CIDOC, in a brochure titled "Developments in International Museum and Cultural Heritage Information Standards," first published in 1993 and updated in July 1995. It is now updated and made available online at http://www.willpowerinfo.myby.co.uk/cidoc/stand2.htm.

- Archival Information Systems Architecture Working Group
- Art & Architecture Thesaurus (AAT)
- Art Information Task Force (AITF)
- Bureau of Canadian Archivists
- Canadian Heritage Information Network (CHIN)
- Clearinghouse on Art Documentation and Computerization
- Committee on Archival Information Exchange (CAIE)
- Common Agenda for History Museums
- Computer Interchange of Museum Information (CIMI)
- Council of Europe Division for Cultural Heritage
- European Commission (EC)
- Getty Art History Information Program (AHIP)/Getty Information Institute
- ICONCLASS Research and Development Group
- Institute for Cultural Memory (Institutul de Memorie Culturala) (CIMEC), Romania
- International Committee for Costume Museums and Collections
- International Committee for Documentation of the International Council of Museums (CIDOC)
- International Committee for Musical Instrument Museums and Collections (CIMCIM)
- International Confederation of Architectural Museums (ICAM)
- International Council of Museums (ICOM)
- International Council on Archives (ICA) Committee on Automation
- International Council on Archives (ICA) Ad Hoc Committee on Descriptive Standards
- International Federation of Library Associations and Institutions (IFLA)

- International Organization for Standardization (ISO)
- Inventaire général des monuments et des richesses artistiques de la France
- Istituto Centrale per il Catalogo e la Documentazione (ICCD)
- Museum Computer Network (MCN)
- MDA (formerly the "Museum Documentation Association")
- National Council on Archives (NCA)
- Network of Art Research Computer Image Systems in Europe (NARCISSE)
- Remote Access to Museum Archives (RAMA)
- Royal Commission on the Historical Monuments of England (RCHME)
- Society of American Archivists (SAA) Standards Board
- Society of American Archivists Working Group on Standards for Archival Description (WGSAD)
- Text Encoding Initiative (TEI)
- Thesaurus Artis Universalis (TAU)
- Thesaurus of Geographic Names (TGN)
- Union List of Artist Names (ULAN)

List of Currently Available Monolingual Lexicons Online

For a list of multilingual lexicons, see the appendix titled "Registered Thesauri on the Survey's Web site" in *Multilingual Access to the Digital European Cultural Heritage—Introduction to the Multilingual Diversity of Europe*, http://www.minervaeurope.org/structure/workinggroups/inventor/multilingua/documents/ReportonMultilingualism0512.pdf.

A.K.A.—"a.k.a." combines the inclusive nature of the World Wide Web and the carefully constructed intellectual links and relationships inherent in the Getty vocabulary tools to provide access to what amounts to a "virtual database" of information. Thanks to this "knowledge navigator," made more efficient because of the years of scholarly work and intellectual integration represented by the Getty vocabulary resources, any Internet user can almost instantaneously access a vast amount of cultural heritage information that would take days or even months of work (and in many cases worldwide travel) to find using traditional research tools.

AMICO—For Rutgers faculty, staff, and students. Image providers.

Archaeology and Architecture—Canadian Centre for Architecture Bilingual Term Lists. These bilingual term lists were developed specifically for the CCA collections. The English terms they contain are based on the AAT; French terms were carefully added after checking use of the terms in the field of architecture. Bilingual term lists include archaeology and architecture. Other vocabulary standards for archaeology are available on the Archaeology Data Service site. These include: Object Type, Object Component, Unit Catalogued, Subject Classification. For further information, contact Louise Beauregard at the Canadian Centre for Architecture.

ARLIS Visual Resources Division—Art Libraries Society of North America (ARLIS-NA). The Art Libraries Society of North America is the professional support group for art libraries and other art collections, including visual resources collections.

Art & Architecture Thesaurus (AAT)— The Art & Architecture Thesaurus is a controlled vocabulary that is used to improve access to cultural heritage information in the global networked environment. AAT was created by the J. Paul Getty Trust; the AAT is a thesaurus of terms used in the cataloguing and indexing of art, architecture, artifactual, and archival materials. In addition to broader, narrower, and related terms, it contains cross-references, alternative terms, United Kingdom English equivalent terms, source information, and history and scope notes in a thesaurus format. The AAT was developed from numerous existing terminologies, and includes the vocabulary from the Revised Nomenclature, which is widely used in Canadian museums. It is currently available only in English. As the AAT is useful as a controlled vocabulary for recording and retrieval of data in object, bibliographic, and visual databases, it is of interest to a wide community of information professionals such as research librarians, historians, archivists, curators, cataloguers, and collections managers. The Canadian Heritage Information Network (CHIN) recommends the use of the AAT for museums with broad humanities collections. The AAT (with CHIN's addition of 2,600 French language equivalents) is a multifaceted thesauri. It is the control vocabulary for the type, technique, and material authority files in the digital database. Art and Architecture Thesaurus: http://shiva.pub.getty.edu/aat_browser/. AAT Online also lists thirty-three subfacets. The thirty-three subfacets of the AAT structure, which could be considered "primary categories," include such terms as object genres, visual works, processes and techniques, and information forms.

Artcyclopedia links to artist entries on museum Web sites—Dictionaries and Encyclopedias.

Art History Resources Rutgers Art Library Web Resource Guide to research resources maintained by Sara Harrington.

Art History Webmasters is an organization promoting Web sites for the visual arts. The Web site includes a directory of art history departments.

Art Images for College Teaching (AICT)—Image Providers.

Artists in Canada—Artists in Canada, compiled and maintained by the National Gallery of Canada Library, is a bilingual union list that identifies the location of documentation files on Canadian artists. Libraries and art galleries across Canada have contributed biographical information and lists of their documentation files to create this resource which contains information for over 42,700 artists. Each record includes artists' names; brief biographical information on the artist, such as birth and/or death dates; place of birth and/or death; artist technique; and some name variants. Bilingual. Also available in print.

ArtLex—Art Dictionary—Dictionaries and Encyclopedias.

Artnet Artists, materials and styles—Dictionaries and Encyclopedias.

ARTstor—Image Providers.

Askart—artist and museum directory—Other Directories.

Base de données Thésaurus—This architecture thesaurus was developed by the direction de l'Architecture et du Patrimoine of the French Ministère de la Culture et de la Communication. It contains 1,135 terms to describe architectural works. The thesaurus is used for indexing the material in the French national heritage database, Mérimée. It includes definitions and usage notes. The thesaurus also includes English and Italian equivalents. The thesaurus is multilingual, but the interface is available only in French.

Beazley Archive: http://www.beazley.ox.ac.uk.

BibleGateway—Look up passages in different translations—Dictionaries and Encyclopedias.

British Museum Materials Thesaurus—This thesaurus, developed by the British Museum based on the materials found in their collection, covers a very wide range of materials. It has three top-level terms: organic, inorganic, and processed material. Available in English only. Materials.

British Museum Object Names Thesaurus—Originally set up as an internal reference tool for the British Museum collection, this thesaurus of object names reflects the nature of the British Museum collections. However, other museums have found it to be a useful resource. Available online in English only. Object Names.

Building Materials Thesaurus—Construction materials (e.g., granite, steel, clay) for monuments relating to built and buried heritage. Available in English only.

Canadian Geographical Names Data Base (CGNDB)—The CGNDB is maintained by Natural Resources Canada to store names for Canadian geographic features, including populated places, administrative areas, and water and terrain features (such as lakes, mountains). Museums may use the CGNDB to help with the consistent naming of Canadian geographic names in their collections databases. The CGNDB provides Canadian place names to a more detailed level than Thesaurus of Geographic Names (TGN); museums may wish to use it in parallel with TGN. Bilingually available online.

Canadian Heritage Information Network (CHIN) collections management software review examined seven areas of several commercially available programs.

Catholic Encyclopedia—Dictionaries and Encyclopedias.

Catholic Online (Saints): http//saints.catholic.org/stsindex.html.

CDWA: Categories for the Description of Works of Art—Image Metadata Standards.

Chenhall's lexicon is a controlled vocabulary created for artifacts; it is useful as a vocabulary with relationships. Generally speaking, if it is a man-made object, there is a way to classify it under Chenhall's system. In databases where relationships can be established, culturally or technically specific terms can be linked to Chenhall terms.

CIMI's release of the Guide to Best Practice: Dublin Core.

Cleveland Museum of Art: http://www.rediscov.com/redcleve/page.htm.

College Art Association—Supports teaching and scholarship in the visual arts.

Columbia Gazetteer—Thesauri.

Conservation & Art Materials Dictionary—Dictionaries and Encyclopedias.

Contemporary Artists (the-artists.org)—Thesauri.

David Rumsey Map Collection—on Luna Insight Platform: historic maps, searchable database, maps.

Defense Visual Information Center: http://www.dodmedia.osd.mil/dvic/.

Diacritical Marks—Other.

Dictionary of Art/Bridgeman: http://www.groveart.com.

Dictionary of Art Historians—Dictionaries and Encyclopedias.

Dublin Core Metadata Initiative.

Encyclopedia.com from Electric Library—Dictionaries and Encyclopedias.

Encyclopedia Mythica: http://www.pantheon.org/mythica.

English Dictionaries Available through Rutgers University Libraries—Dictionaries and Encyclopedias.

Gazetteer of British Place Names (helpful for places not in TGN but last county changes not included)—Thesauri.

German English Dictionary—German.

Getty Vocaulary Tools (ULAN, AAT, TGN)—Thesauri. The Getty Information Institute (GII), previously known as the Art History Information Program (AHIP), an institution of the J. Paul Getty Trust, has developed three important vocabulary resources. The Art & Architecture Thesaurus (AAT) is a ninety-thousand-term structured guide to vocabulary describing art and architecture. Links to two hundred thousand names referring to one hundred thousand artists, and is taken from the files of Getty projects. The Thesaurus of Geographic Names contains three hundred thousand hierarchically linked place names in vernacular languages and anglicized forms. AHIP also sponsored the Thesaurus Artis Universalis (TAU), a comittee under the Commitee International d'Histoire de l'Art (CIHA), which examined and recommended standards for developing databases of biographic information on artists and for creating historical-geographic databases. The Getty Information Institute also worked with the Architectural Drawings Advisory Group and the Foundation for Documents of Arhcitecture to establish guidelines for the catalogue.

Grove Dictionary of Art/Access restricted to Rutgers University faculty, staff, and students— Dictionaries and Encyclopedias.

Hargrett Library Rare Map Collection, University of Georgia—Historic Maps of United States—Maps.

Historical Atlas of Europe—Maps.

Historical Gazeteer of Great Britain—Maps.

Historical Maps and Atlases—Page of links to hisorical maps at the Jewish Resource Center at Hebrew University of Jerusalem. Numerous links to biblical and Jewish history maps but the site includes many links to other areas and periods.

Historical Maps of Great Britain—Maps.

ICONCLASS, the premier iconographic system, was developed in Europe at the University of Leiden, Netherlands. It contains nine primary categories as follows: 0 abstract, nonrepresentational art; 1 religion and magic; 2 nature; 3 human being, man in general; 4 society, civilization, culture; 5 abstract ideas and concepts; 6 history; 7 Bible; 8 literature; 9 classical mythology and ancient history. Iconclass is the control vocabulary for the subject authority file in the digital database. Thesauri. ICONCLASS: http://iconclass.nl.

Image Metadata Standards.

Images on the World Wide Web—Image Providers.

Index of Christian Art—Indexes.

INSCRIPTION—The INSCRIPTION site, maintained by MDA on behalf of the Forum on Information Standards in Heritage (FISH), provides access to word lists to be used for compiling archaeological and architectural heritage inventories. Archaeology and Architecture.

Integrated Taxonomic Information System—Canadian Version (ITIS *ca). ITIS is a database created by an international partnership of agencies and taxonomic specialists. ITIS provides information on species names and their hierarchical classification; it includes "documented taxonomic information of flora and fauna from both aquatic and terrestrial habitats." For each scientific name, ITIS includes "the authority (author and date), taxonomic rank, associated synonyms and vernacular names where available, a unique taxonomic serial number, data source information (publications, experts, etc.) and data quality indicators." CHIN is implementing ITIS as a search tool in Artefacts Canada: Natural Sciences. Natural Sciences. "About ITIS," June 2001. Available online at www.itis.usda.gov/info.html.

International Terminology Working Group (ITWG)—The International Terminology Working Group, an informal association of cultural heritage information professionals from several countries, originally grew out of the Thesaurus Artis Universalis (TAU) committee of the Comité International de l'Histoire de l'Art (CIHA). Members of this group have met, usually once a year in Europe, to report on their various projects and activities in the field of cultural heritage terminology. At the general meeting of the International Terminology Working Group held at the University of Amsterdam in September 1996 on the occasion of the twenty-ninth CIHA conference, members of the group reported on terminology projects underway in Canada, England, France, Germany, Italy, The Netherlands, Spain, and the United States. Although most of these projects have taken the AAT as their point of departure, other sources, such as ICONCLASS, or an institution's own collections (as at the Victoria & Albert Museum in London), are also being used.

Language Aids—Dictionaries and Encyclopedias.

LC Thesaurus for Graphic Materials I: Subject Terms (TGM I)—Thesauri.

LC Thesaurus for Graphic Materials II (TGM II)—Thesauri.

Lexicon Iconographicum Mythologiae Classicae (LIMC). It is considered to be the ultimate source of subject classification for classical mythology and is profusely illustrated. This tool is only available in print form and requires the entire set of volumes to be used correctly. Lexicon. Iconographicum Mythologiae Classicae (information only): http://www.rzuser.uni-heidelberg.de/~m99/.

Library of Congress Online Catalog—Elisabeth Betz Parker of the Library of Congress Picture and Photograph Collection published Thesaurus for Graphic Materials, a pioneering work for subject indexing of nonbibliographic materials. The Thesaurus for Graphic Materials is now also available online, and includes many principles and references on image indexing, including "of" and "about" guidelines. The Library of Congress also supported the subject description of graphic materials. Indexes. The Library of Congress says, "As other Metadata formats become standard usage in particular communities, we must be prepared to do the same. There has been some work with the Government Information Locator

Service (GLIS) and its adaptability to MARC. The hope is that eventually these adaptations can be handled by machine with minimum staff intervention." See also what David Bearman said at the Library of Congress. Library of Congress subject headings have provided usable controlled vocabulary for libraries, and are a useful tool for building a vocabulary with relationships. Because this system is based on an extremely wide field of terms (i.e., those about which books have been written), it is very useful for generally known terms. Culturally specific or technically specific terms may be lacking. Thesauri.

Luna Imaging—Image Providers.

Maps of Islamic Development—University of Penn Site—Maps.

MDA's FISHEN—Forum on Information Standards in Heritage (England). MDA Archaeological Objects Thesaurus.

Names of archaeological objects (e.g., amulet, flask, tile) that can be recovered from archaeological fieldwork. Available in English only. Archaeology and Architecture.

National Gallery of Art Slide Library: http://www.nga.gov/library/slidesearch.htm.

National Museum of American Art: http://nmaa-ryder.si.edu/study/index.html.

Osshe Historical & Cultural Atlas—Shockwave plugin needed for some maps, which are interactive. Maps.

Oxford English Dictionary for Rutgers Community—Dictionaries & Encyclopedias.

Panoramic Maps Collection Smithsonian Institution Site—Historic Maps— Maps.

Princeton Index to Christian Art: http://www.princeton.edu/~ica/indexca.html. Regarding Metadata standards.

Religious Objects's User's Guide and Terminology. The result of joint effort of French and Canadian researchers of a project under the Canada-France Accord, this work is a pilot project for the bringing together of the French and Canadian methodologies for analyzing data and for data entry and management. Includes a guide that explains the method for data entry and provides a standardized, hierarchical authority list of over three hundred terms for religious objects. Bilingual print version available for sale from CHIN. Object Names.

Revised Nomenclature for Museum Cataloging: A Revised and Expanded Edition of Robert G. Chenhall's System for Classifying Man-Made Objects. The Revised Nomenclature, published by the American

Association for State and Local History, is a hierarchical classification system (and partial term list) for man-made objects (excludes natural history objects). Nomenclature is organized on the basis of the original function of the object. This revision as well as the original Nomenclature are widely used in history museums, including many Canadian museums. It has a partial lexicon; definitions for major artifact categories are provided. A few of the classification terms are defined as well. Revised Nomenclature was used as a terminology source for the Art & Architecture Thesaurus. The Revised Nomenclature is available in print, in English only. Object Names.

Robert Baron's SWAP Project Building. A small museum database from the bottom up. Other.

Rutgers University Libraries Reference Sources Dictionaries, Encyclopedias, Maps etc.—Dictionaries and Encyclopedias.

Rutgers University Libraries Web site—Indexes.

Rutgers VRC Authority Lists for Type, Subject, etc. (need password)—Thesauri.

Society of Architectural Historians.

Thesaurus for Graphic Materials II: Genre and Physical Characteristic Terms (TGM II). TGM II was created by the Library of Congress Prints and Photographs Division as a companion to TGM I. It provides headings for categories of material—by genre (portraits, etc.), by vantage point, method of representation, production technique or version, marking, shape or size, intended purpose, characteristics of the image's creator, or publication status. Terms denoting artistic movements and styles are not included. Available in English only. Multifaceted.

Thesaurus for Graphic Materials: http://lcweb.loc.gov/rr/print/tgm1/.

Thesaurus of Geographic Names (TGN)—The Getty Thesaurus of Geographic Names (TGN) is a structured vocabulary developed primarily for the field of art history, but with the potential for wide applications in related disciplines such as archaeology, history, and geography. The TGN is the only available geographic resource that is both hierarchical and global in scope. The TGN contains nearly 1 million place names representing approximately nine hundred thousand places. The TGN was created by the J. Paul Getty Trust. The TGN is a "structured vocabulary containing around 1,000,000 names and other information about places. The TGN includes all continents and nations of the modern political world, as well as historical places. It includes physical features and administrative entities, such as cities and nations. The emphasis in TGN is on places important for art and architecture." The terms in the TGN are multilingual, but the database interface is available only in English. Place names "About the TGN." Available online at www.getty.edu/research/-tools/vocabulary/tgn/about.html.

Thesaurus of Graphic Materials I: Subject Terms (TGM I)—TGM I was created by the Library of Congress Prints and Photographs Division to support both cataloguing and retrieval needs. It is used for subject indexing of graphical materials, including historical photographs, architectural drawings, artwork, and so on. Includes a controlled vocabulary for describing "a broad range of subjects depicted in such materials, including activities, objects, types of people, events, and places." Proper names of people, organizations, events, and geographic places are not included. Available in English only. Multifaceted. "TGM I—Summary of Features." August 2000. Available online at lcweb.loc.gov/rr/print/tgm1 /ia.html.

Thesaurus of Monument Types—A thesaurus containing terms for types of monuments (e.g., cathedral, museum, school) relating to the built and buried heritage in England. Created by English Heritage for the National Monuments Record. Available in English only. Archaeology and Architecture.

UC Berkeley. SPIRO: http://shanana.berkeley.edu/spiro/.

UC Santa Cruz: http://slides-www.ucsc.edu/Slidecat.

UCSD Roger Slide Search—Image Providers.

Union List of Artist Names (ULAN)—The ULAN is used as an authority file or data value standard in the documentation (cataloguing, indexing, and description) of cultural heritage information. Building on consensus among its contributing projects and upon ranking according to scholarly usage, the ULAN establishes an "entry form" or heading that can be used as a collective device or point of reference for all of the associated data relating to a particular artist or architect, including variant names, biographical information, and bibliographic citations. Union List of Artists' Names. Thesauri . ULAN was created by the J. Paul Getty Trust. ULAN is a "structured vocabulary that contains around 220,000 names and other information about artists. The coverage of the ULAN is from antiquity to the present, and the scope is global. ULAN includes artist names. The ULAN can include the vernacular, English, other languages, natural order, inverted order, or nicknames. There is no "preferred" name identified in the ULAN; instead, many variants of the name are provided. The artist names in ULAN are multilingual, but the database interface is available only in English. Names, relationships, locations (for birth, death, and activity), important dates, and notes are included. "About the ULAN." Available online at www.getty.edu/research/tools/vocabulary /ulan/about.html.

University of Texas Map Collection—Excellent site for current maps of counties and regions; find link on left to historical maps (includes 1923 Sheperds' Maps).

Uptravel World Maps—Includes historical maps (navigate by links in yellow box). Maps.

Visual Resources Association Core Categories/VISION Project: http://www.oberlin.edu/~art/vra/vision.html.

Visual Resources Facilities Webpage—Some of the more recent Visual Resources facilities are included at this site. A plan and numerous photos represent each facility. Includes pictures of the Rutgers VRC. Other.

Vocabulary of Basic Terms for Cataloguing Costume—A multilingual (English, French, and German) vocabulary of costume terminology, created by the ICOM International Committee for the Museums and Collections of Costume. Includes drawings to help museums identify objects and properly classify them. Object Names.

VRA—Visual Resources Association (Greater New York Chapter). The VRA is an international association of professionals supporting visual resources collections with publications, annual meetings, a listserve, and so on. The site includes links to copyright pages and data standards. VRA Core 3.0. Image Metadata Standards.

WadeGiles/Pinyon Comparison Charts—Chinese.

International Council of Museums (ICOM), "Statutes," Code of Professional Ethics

The version quoted below is correct for 2005. There is an updated version (2006) which can be found at http://icom.museum/ethics.html#intro.

ARTICLE 1.2. MUSEUM

A museum is defined in article 2 paragraph 2 of the statutes of the International Council of Museums as "a non-profit making, permanent institution in the service of society and of its acquires, conserves, researches, communicates and exhibits, for purposes of study, education and enjoyment, material evidence of people and their environment."

ARTICLE 2.5 PERSONNEL

The governing body has a special obligation to ensure that the museum has staff sufficient in both number and kind so that the museum is able to meet its responsibilities. The size of the staff and its nature will depend on the size of the museums, its collections and its responsibilities. However, proper arrangement should be made for the museum to meet its obligations in relation to the care of the collections, public access and serious, research and security.... The governing body should recognize the diverse nature of the museum profession and the wide range of specialization that it now encompasses, including conservator/restorers, scientists, museum's education service personnel, registrars and computer specialists, security service managers, etc. It should ensure that both makes appropriate set for such specialists where required and that such specialized personnel are properly recognized full members of the professional staff in all respects.

ARTICLE 2.6 EDUCATIONAL AND COMMUNITY ROLE OF THE MUSEUM

By definition, a museum is an institution in the service of society and of its development, and is generally open to the public.

The museum should take every opportunity to develop its role as an educational resource used by all sections of the population or specialized group that the museum is intended to serve. Where appropriate in relation to the museums program and responsibilities, specialized staff with training and skills in museum education are likely to be required for this purpose.

The museum has an important duty to attract new and wider audiences within all levels of the community, locality or group that the museum aims to serve.

ARTICLE 2.7 PUBLIC ACCESS

The general public should have access to the displays during reasonable hours and for regular periods. The museums should also offer the public reasonable access to members of staff by appointment or other arrangements, and full access to information about collections, subject to any necessary restrictions for reasons of confidentiality or security as discussed in paragraph 7.3 below.

ARTICLE 7.3 CONFIDENTIALITY

Members of the museums profession must protect all confidential information relating to the source of material owned by or loaned to the museums, as well as information concerning the security arrangements of the museum, . . . there is a special responsibility to respect the personal confidences contained in oral history or other personal material. . . . [persons] have the right to remain anonymous if they so choose. This right should be respected where it has been promised.

A Partial List of Museum Database Programs

The following list includes some of the more popular collections management systems. For an in-depth review of some of the software listed see "MDA Software Survey", http://www.mda.org.uk/softover.htm. Most of the software listed does not support a truly multilingual setting defined as using parallel columns for each language. Some do enable data entry in Unicode.

Access
Accession
ADMUSE
ARGUS
ARTchive
Artefact (formerly CMB Storager)
Artifact
Artsystem
ArtWatch
askSAM
Bulldog, now Documentum
CALM2000
Catalyst for Windows
Cinebase
CMB Storager (is now Artefact)
Collection
Collections-Museum
Cumulus
Datapoint
Digital Link
EmbARK has become part of Gallery Systems
Epoch
FileMaker Pro
4th Dimension
GCOLL
GENCAT

Heritage Sentinel
History Database
House of Images
IBM Digital Library
IDEALIST
IMC Modules
In arte Plus (Portuguese & Spanish)
INCA
Inmagic DB/Textworks
KE Texpress (KE Emu)
Logos Flow
MCMS
MicroMARC:AMC
Micromusee
Minaret
MINISIS
MIS
MODES for Windows
MODES Plus MIS
Multi MIMSY 2000
Museum System, The
MUSIMS, and Index+ CMS
Oracle
PastPerfect
Re:Discovery
REGIS
Snap! for Windows
SNAP/MultiMIMSY
STAR
Status/M
Virage
Virtual Collections

Questionnaire for Museums with Answers

After filling in the questionnaire form, the researchers then sent the responses to the author, who subsequently summarized the findings in a grading system, which is included in this book, see Grading System for Museum's Size in chapter 3. This grading system should be used as a tool to define the size of museums and to propose the stages of computerization recommended for a museum of this size. The grade takes into account the level of computerization in the museum at present and then is able to propose the course of action for the specific museums. Below is an example of a completed questionnaire.

The Babylonian Jewry Heritage Center
Name of researcher: Danny Goldman
Address: 76, Stern Street, Kiryat Ono, 55602, Israel
E-mail: dannyg1@netvision.net.il
Field of expertise: Architectural History
Is this your first visit to this museum? yes
If not, what has been your past over all experience when visiting this museum?
Information pertaining to museum visited
Name of museum: The Babylonian Jewry Heritage Center
Place (city, state): Or-Yehuda Israel
Address: 83, Ben-Porath Ave. Or-Yehuda, 60251
Type of museum (archaeology, modern art, mixed, etc.): Ethnology, Heritage, Historical.
Publicly funded/state run: Run By: Ministry of Education, Or-Yehuda Municipality, contribution, and tickets.
Size of museum: 800 SQM, now in construction of additional 800 SQM.
Number of objects in collection: Photographs ~ 6,000, objects ~ 5,000, documents ~ 2,000.
Number of visitors per year: 25,000
Square meters of campus: ~ 6,000 SQM
How much does it cost to enter the museum (ticket cost in dollars): 15 NIS per person in a group (guided) 12 NIS per person not in a group, unguided.

Is the museum:
Educational/ pure exhibition hall Both
Elitist/populist
Family oriented/group oriented/single-visitor oriented: Group and single-visitor oriented.
How many times a year do you frequent the museum: Less then once a year.
At what times of the year did you frequent the museum:
vacations/free time/ weekends
What was your average length of stay in the museum
20 minutes/2 hours/4 hours?
What was your favorite exhibit and why? Photographs.
If you could prepare an exhibit, what subject matter would interest you most? Interesting buildings, public and residential.
Does the museum have guided tours: Yes.
Are the guides
Older women/young guides All women between 24–40, all paid. One male volunteer.
Are they paid or volunteer staff: All paid except for one volunteer.
Do they offer audio guides (handheld devices)? No.
Is there a gift shop at the museum: Yes.
Are there food areas in the museum: No, planning on adding a food area in the future.
Is there parking: Yes.
Is the museum accessible for the disabled? Yes.
How many publications a year does the museum produce: 2 booklets average a year, plus publications of the research institute.
Are they sold exclusively by the gift shop? The booklets are distributed free to members, + contributors who are mentioned in the booklet, + to universities, libraries, and museums.
Information pertaining to the museum's use of computers
Does this museum make use of computers: Yes.
If yes, which of the users and which programs
For the curators
Everyday work needs: MS Office programs.
Database of collections (Information pertaining to the holdings in the collection): in the process of conversion from manual DB to digital DB.
Home access for curators work (this you will need to ask a curator): No.
Other
For the public
Kiosks in the galleries: No
If yes, what content/programs
Internet
Internet access in the museum: No.
From the home (what is the URL address): Yes, URL: www.babylonjewry
.org.il

Multimedia: In the making.

Virtual exhibits: In the making.

Database of collections (Information pertaining to the holdings in the collection): "TAMUZ" application; database of images and scanned documents.

Other

Which if any for the above answers can be found into the site

Images: Yes.

Rights and reproductions—does the museums sell image rights to the public

If yes, how much does it cost to have a visitor purchase the rights to use in a doctoral thesis: An image without publication: $10, with publication $30, no charge for a PhD thesis.

Can the image be sent as a digital image via the Internet (as a jpeg, tiff, etc.): No.

Report of Experiments Recycling Data in the Museum

INTRODUCTION

The goal was to investigate the most time and money efficient manner of gaining digital information.

SIX EXPERIMENTS

There were six experiments performed, all with the intention of learning the most efficient manner of accumulating digitized information in a generic format for conversion to the final database. The experiments included:

1. Recycling edited and translated texts from texts produced for wall labels.
2. Recycling edited and translated texts from a Word document prepared for a multimedia exhibit.
3. Recycling images from scans and texts originally prepared for the publication of catalogues.
4. Using OCR for transferring information for a hard copy of a catalogue to a Word file.
5. Comparing the above to entering data straight from the catalogue cards.
6. Using Microsoft Access to turn the tables on their axis.

GUIDELINES FOR WORKING IN FLAT TABLES: EXCEL AS THE GENERIC TABLE

The decisions to use Excel as a flat table was made with the consultation of systems, the local distributors, and support company for the database. Since they would be doing the future conversions, they were consulted and they recommended Excel. The setup of these tables was to resemble the flat tables that resulted from the first experiment performed when converting Microsoft Access files from the registrar's office. The filed names all appeared in the first column with the data in the next column. This decision applied to the first four experiments listed earlier.

GUIDELINES FOR WORKING IN FLAT TABLES: FIELD NAMES

As all information was to end up in the same database, the fields were studied and compared with the catalogue cards which had been filled in by hand over the last thirty-five years. Using both these sources a list of fields was assembled. This list became more finely tuned as time progressed. In the last stages a volunteer was asked to unify all the files assembled so that one master list of fields was used. This decision affected the information in the first four experiments listed earlier.

GUIDELINES FOR WORKING IN FLAT TABLES: IMAGES FILE NAMES

All images were to be associated with either the department number (Judaica) or the registration number (all other departments). This was possible using a program called Cumulus. Cumulus helped catalogue assets (image files) by creating a thumbnail of the image, saving the asset's original file name, and allowing information to be added into a field called "record name" which was the unique department or registration number. The minimum resolution for an image was set at 5 × 7 " at 300 dpi saved as a tiff file (1500 × 2100 pixels) with the average color image size around 5 MB.

CONCLUSIONS FOR EXPERIMENT 1—TEXTS PRODUCED FOR WALL LABELS

(Permanent exhibit labels—one thousand objects)

Labels found in the museum near art objects as labeling texts are edited and translated. This is a very expensive process, and the recycling of this information has great importance as the texts produced for wall labels have gone through an editing process and are considered "clean" texts. It was also assumed that the information would be found on disks or some computer in the museum. The permanent exhibit was chosen as a first source for the wall labels. Unfortunately the files were not found for the permanent exhibit assembled some fifteen years previously.

The typist of the department performed the data entry. This was significant as her familiarity with the terminology as well as the curators in charge of each object enabled her to ask questions and get answers from these curators when it was necessary.

The hard copy of the labels written fifteen years before was saved in a file separated by gallery spaces. This served as the source for the texts.

The Excel table consisted of four columns. The first column was intended for field names, the next Hebrew label data, the following held English label data and the last held the unique number associated with the data, which in this case was the department number for the objects. (See Table VII.2 A Word Document Opened in Excel and Mapped to Fields.)

The texts were typed into the appropriate fields. At the end of this process, an additional file was added to associate the objects to the correct gallery space, termed temporary storage since each object has an additional space in the storage rooms in the case of a war or for purposes of changing exhibits.

The advantages for Experiment 1 were as follows: The information found on the labels was "clean, having already been edited and translated."

The images associated with the unique number required this "label." It was enough information for use by external departments although not for the department responsible for the object.

There were also disadvantages. Because the information was written some fifteen years before, there were discoveries or changes that the curators had since discovered or researched. This new information wasn't found within the label texts but rather in the catalogue cards.

As many as a third of the labels did not have the object's department number on them. This made the work of their digitization very difficult. The museum's policy had been to do away with the department number on the labels, as it served no purpose for the visitors' knowledge. We found this not to be the case because when a visitor came in to ask for information about a specific object, it was very time consuming to find the information without the department number. The curators had to be consulted, and the missing information had to be supplied.

The curators, having examined the results of this experiment, wanted to know more about the object and wanted to have all the information they had noted on the catalogue cards. This was the catalyst for Experiment 4.

CONCLUSIONS FOR EXPERIMENT 2—TEXT DATA FROM WORD DOCUMENT

(The Cycles Multimedia Word files—three hundred objects)

When a curator within the museum prepares texts for catalogues or for other publicly displayed texts, he/she always begins in Microsoft Word. As long as there is a consistent order to the texts, there is reason to believe that the texts can be moved from prose to a table format. The information chosen for this experiment was from the virtual exhibit that was on view in the galleries using Macromedia Director as the program base. The original texts that were edited and translated were in Microsoft Word. As the texts were in a consistent order (e.g., name of object, city, country, year, material, technique, photo copyright, descriptive texts, etc.), these were the first texts tested.

The Word document was changed so that each new field was on its own line. This was done by a search and replace command for all commas.

The advantages to this experiment were as follows: The information found in the Word files was very "clean, having been edited and translated."

There was a high-resolution image for each object prepared for the multimedia program.

The information was written very recently and was up to date with curatorial research. This newly corrected information was not found in the catalogue cards.

The object texts had all been associated with the unique numbers, that is, the department number and the registration number

There was bibliographic information noted in the text; such information was not found in any other sources.

Unfortunately, there were some disadvantages. After the texts were assembled in what could be seen as a single column or table, it was copied and pasted into Excel. Each line fell into its own data cell. Parallel to this column, a field name column was constructed with the name of the field names repeating at equal intervals. There was a lot of cleaning up work to make certain that all the data fell into the right field spaces.

The curators wanted to know more about the object and wanted to have all the information they had noted on the catalogue cards. This was the catalyst for Experiment 4.

CONCLUSIONS FOR EXPERIMENT 3—IMAGES AND TEXTS FROM CATALOGUES

(The Modern Art Department—eight hundred objects)

The objective of the experiment was to "recycle" information that was used in producing the printed catalogue and to insert this information into the database. The original intention was to use both the images and texts, but as the images were in their final state and the text was to undergo a last set of corrections, the images were treated first.

The goal was to see if this would afford the museum the opportunity to save time and money in adding information into its database. The underlying understanding was that the information ascertained from the publisher was the highest quality images with the most "finished" texts (edited, translated).

There were nine hundred images from the catalogue. The six months spent trying to get the information from the publishing house is not included in our calculations (a special thank you goes to the curator for being catalyst in making this process a successful one).

Storage and recycling of publication data is of the utmost importance. The highest quality texts (often edited and translated) as well as the highest quality images are used in the museum publications. During the fall of 2000, a project was begun in order to run a test case on the Arturo Schwatz catalogue. During the next six months, a great deal of effort went into receiving the twelve CDs of the eight hundred images from the publishing house. The texts were to be supplied by the Publications Department after final textual corrections were to be added. It was decided that these texts would be sent in a PDF format.

Over a period of two months the eight hundred scans were converted from the Mac CD, identified with the registration number, catalogued and saved. The work order was as follows:

A list of published works with their artist name, title, and registration number was received from the Registrar's office.

A hard copy of the catalogue was received and the registration numbers were marked inside in pencil.

In PhotoShop, the scans were changed from EPS format to tiff.

In Cumulus, images were catalogued by registration number.

TABLE VII.1 Comparing cost and time of information recycled from catalogue vs. source material entered in the museum

Number of images 900	Information received from catalogue	Entered source material in museum
Cost	$250 (CD) + $1,000 (staff)	$4,500
Time	1 month	2 months
Storage	$2,400	$2,400
Total	$3,650	$6,900
Total saved	$3,250 (and 1 month)	

As requested by the curator, each file was saved with the artist name, title of work. and registration number.

The files were placed on the server, as requested by the curator, in an alphabetical filing system.

The scans would then have many secondary uses: selling information (images and texts), planning exhibit, condition reports, and so on.

To date the text files have not been received.

The advantages to this experience were multiple. The information found in the catalogue was very "clean, having been edited and translated." There was a high-resolution image for many objects. The information was written very recently and was up to date with curatorial research. This newly corrected information was not found in the catalogue cards. There was bibliographic information noted in the text, information not found in any other sources.

This work proved that the recycling information saves the museum money (See Table VII.1). The scans cost the museum one-half of their projected costs in time and workforce than had the work been done from scratch. The Publications Department might request that a CD be received at the end of every project. This CD would be stored at the Visual Resources Department where it was duplicated and a copy sent to Collections Management Project Team for cataloguing and storage of information on the server. A contract with the publishing house should include the museum's right to receive a CD at the end of the publication process. If registration numbers are missing, the curator must include a catalogue with the registration numbers marked within to aid in the cataloguing process.

There were disadvantages. The object texts and images were not associated with the unique numbers: the department number or the registration number. There was a lot of research necessary to fill in this information so as to tag the data correctly.

The final data resided in a Mac file at the printing house. There was a lot of legwork necessary to reclaim the files and to convert them to a PC format.

CONCLUSIONS FOR EXPERIMENT 4—OCR OF A CATALOGUE

In order to quickly enter handwritten texts or catalogues that were not already digitized in the museum's computers, an English-Hebrew OCR (optical character recognition) program called Ligatures was used. This program was chosen after testing the ability of various programs to translate the image of a Hebrew document to texts. It was found that there were many programs that were able to do this work in English so this was not the consideration. After trying many different DPIs for the scans, it was decided to use 300 DPI when using the OCR.

There were no advantages.

Disadvantages were limited. With all the experiments, there was an 80 percent correction level of translation form the image to the text. That can be translated into the following: for every five-letter word one letter was wrong. For this reason it was decided to type in the information form scratch rather then use OCR. It was also concluded that the effort of tracking down the original texts was worthwhile (i.e., when dealing with labels to find the publisher who did the work, etc.)

CONCLUSIONS FOR EXPERIMENT 5—DATA ENTRY FROM CATALOGUE CARDS

The main difference between the information for the label and the catalogue cards was that the public viewed the label after the information was edited and translated, but the catalogue card information was written, as previously noted, for the curator and was neither meant for the public nor edited and translated. These catalogue cards appeared in either English or Hebrew, depending on the curator who catalogued the objects.

According to the curator, it was very advantageous that the information found in the catalogue cards was the most updated. True data entry should be done by this method as there is a unique card per object and all its true information can be found there. The information was written very recently and was up to date with curatorial research.

There were two distinct disadvantages. The catalogue cards are handwritten and hard to decipher and therefore a staff member from the department familiar with the handwriting and terminology was necessary for the task. The newly corrected information found on the labels was most often not found on the catalogue card.

CONCLUSIONS FOR EXPERIMENT 6—USING MICROSOFT ACCESS TO TURN THE TABLES FROM EXCEL ON THEIR AXIS

Recycling of textual data is the most useful way to start to build a database. The original textual data found in the museum was always arranged as a list (labels, catalogue entries, etc.). The label lists most often were somewhat uniform by arranging so that every new bit of information appeared on its own line (usually exchanging the comma for a paragraph mark), we were able to assemble a long chain of information in a linear way. This list of data was copied and pasted into Excel. The data were then matched to the appropriate field names in a parallel left column. Table VII.2 is an example of data from Word with each new bit of information on its own line opened in Excel and matched to appropriate fields.

TABLE VII.2   A Word document opened in excel and mapped to fields

Field Name	Data	Unique Number
01DEPT_NUMBER	123/456	123/456
02REGISTRAR_NUMBER	L99.1234	123/456
03OBJECT_NAME	Lamp	123/456
04CITY		123/456
05COUNTRY	Poland	123/456
06ARTIST		123/456
07YEAR	18th century	123/456
08JEWISH_YEAR		123/456
10aFREE_TEXT_HISTORY		123/456
10cFREE_TEXT_RELATED	This lamp is unique in its architectural form.	123/456
10dFREE_TEXT_DESCRIPTIONS		123/456
11MATERIAL	Brass	123/456
12MATERIAL1		123/456
17TECHNIQUE	Cast	123/456
18TECHNIQUE1	Engraved	123/456
21DIMENSIONS_W	29.2	123/456
22DIMENSIONS_H	35	123/456
23DIMENSIONS_L	15.4	123/456
24DIMENSIONS		123/456
25PHOTO_CREDIT	Photo by James Smith	123/456
26IMC	Italian Museum Collection	123/456
27COLLECTION	The Jones Collection	123/456
28COLLECTION_CREDIT	Donated with the contribution of the John Doe, New York, through Friends of the Museum. 1985	123/456
29HALLMARKS		123/456
30STORAGE		123/456
31aEXHIBITION HISTORY		123/456
32ADDITIONAL INFORMATION		123/456
33REGISTRATION		123/456
34INSCRIPTIONS		123/456
35NEGATIVE_ NUMBER		123/456
37BIBLIOGRAPHY_AUTHOR	Benjamin, Kate.	123/456
38BIBLIOGRAPHY_TITLE	The Jones Collection Catalogue	123/456
39aCATALOGUE_NUMBER		123/456
39aSCREEN_NUMBER	154	123/456
39BIBLIOGRAPHY_PUBL	The Museum, 1987.	123/456
40BIBLIOGRAPHY_PG_	No. 154, p. 206.	123/456
41BIBLIOGRAPHY_LANG_	English	123/456

This flat table was an important first step to the database (see Experiment 2 for a similar process till this point). The next step was to turn this table on its axis so that it would resemble a database in its final form. A database should have its field names on the top row and its data beneath with a unique number at the start of each new row. Microsoft Access has a very nice way of doing this work. The steps are as follows.

Check the Excel table field names very carefully so that the field names are exact and consistent throughout.

In Microsoft Access open a new file. Then choose file/get external data/ import. Choose the Excel file. Make sure to check the box; the first row contains column headings.

FIGURE VII.1 Microsoft Access file dialogue showing "first row contains column headings"

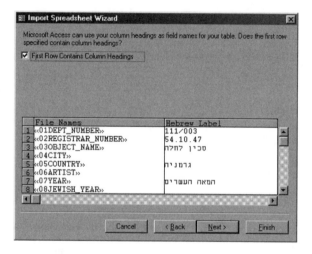

Save as a table.

FIGURE VII.2 Table in Microsoft Access

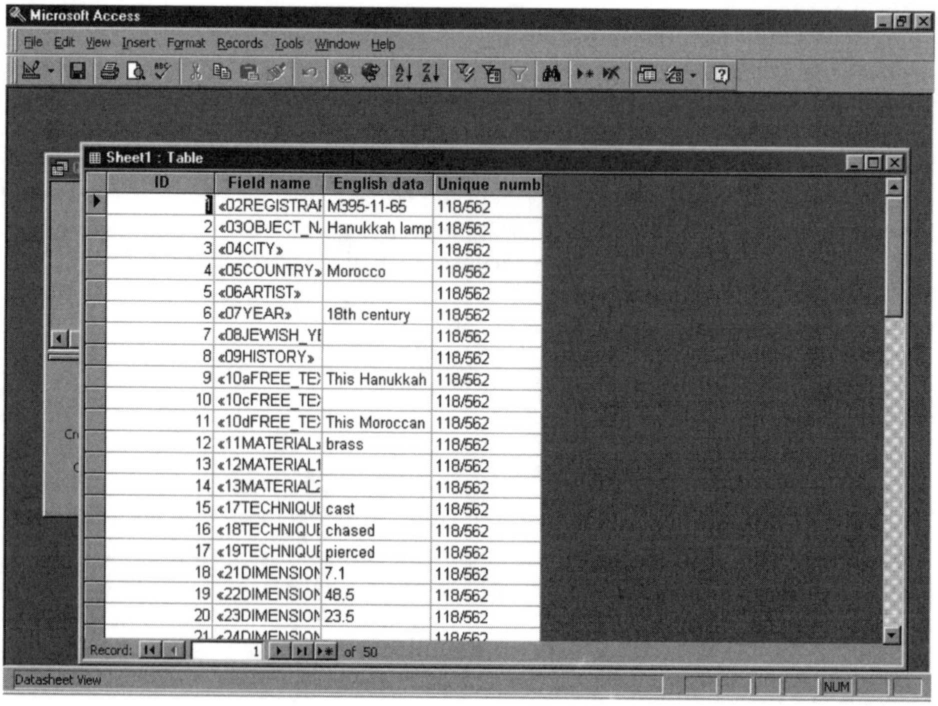

Choose query/new/design view. Choose the new table. Choose Query/ cross tab query. Assemble the data information so that the column heading, row headings, and data values are arranged on a new axis.

FIGURE VII.3 Microsoft Access screen showing heading, row headings, and data values

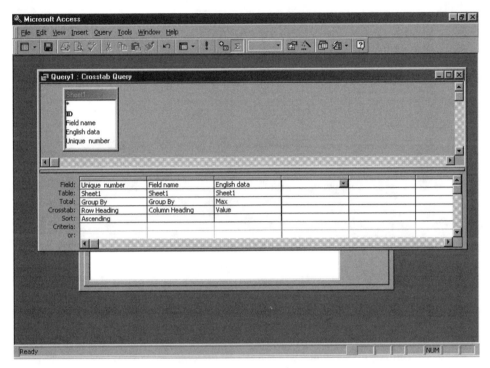

Click on the icon "!". Save result as query. Choose again query/design view and choose query/make table. Choose the resulting query from the last step and use the asterisk to choose all fields as shown below. Click on the icon "!" to make table.

FIGURE VII.4   Microsoft Access window of "make table"

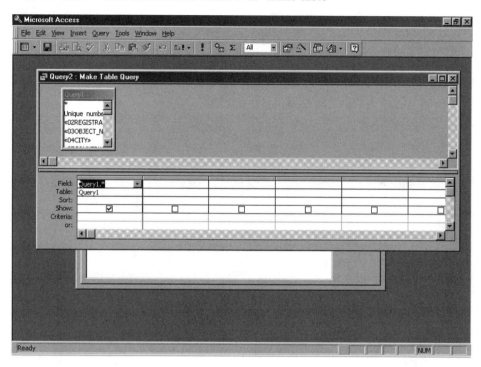

As there were many Excel files that should be attached to the same database, the following step was to append each table to the next. The steps are as follows:

Query—New—Design View. Add the next table you want to append. Insert all the fields (asterisk).

Query—Append Query. Append to the basic table ("English").

Click on the icon "!". If everything is okay, you will see the number of records to be added. If there is a problem, you will have to check the field that does not match.

The resulting information in a true table can now be manipulated in a variety of ways (searches, forms, reports, etc.). Unfortunately, this is quite a complicated process.

Fifteen Worldwide Museum Sites Reviewed

The fifteen Web sites listed were reviewed in 2003 where the focus was to investigate images use and search capabilities in one language. For other tools used in analyzing Web sites, refer to the "Ten Minerva Quality Principles for Grading Web sites" published by Minerva Europe at http://www.minervaeurope .org/publications/tenqualityprinciples.htm.

A pan European report on multilingualism and best practices was recently compiled and edited by Minerva Europe. The author was a contributor and editor of the published report. See the chapter titled "Best Practice Examples of Multilingual Web sites with Thesaurus" in *Multilingual Access to the Digital European Cultural Heritage—Introduction to the Multilingual diversity of Europe*, at http://www.minervaeurope.org/structure/workinggroups /inventor/multilingua/documents/ReportonMultilingualism0512.pdf.

MUSEUM OF ETHNOLOGY, VIENNA

URL: http://www.ethno-museum.ac.at/

Database:

Databases online: No
Computerization statement: N/A
Search capabilities: None
Fields: None, selected fields, artifacts, guided tours
No. of objects in collection: 200,000
Objects online: Selected objects, various categories
Label fields: Basic
Image available: 2 sizes
Image types: Thumbnail, medium, and large: t, m, and l

Copyright for images and texts:

Copyright statement: Yes

Education:

Educational information: N/A

Access and links on site:

How accessed: N/A
Site map: Yes
Bibliography: No
Links: No
Archive material: No

Other computerization projects:

Technical projects online: Highlights, regions
How accessed: Collections

Notes: Highlights, selected collections. Regions, 8 regions, selected objects no choice

LOUVRE, PARIS

URL: http://www.louvre.fr/louvrea.htm

Database:

Databases online: No, only Joconde. See notes.
Computerization statement: Yes
Search capabilities: Partial
Fields: Guided
No. of objects in collection: 70, French museums only
Objects online: Joconde database only
Label fields: Basic and expanded
Image available: 3 sizes
Image types: Thumbnail, medium, and large: t, m, and l

Copyright for images and texts:

Copyright statement: No

Education:

Educational information: Yes

Access and links on-site:

How accessed: Activities, main page
Site map: Yes
Bibliography: No, except shop with search facility
Links: No
Archive material: No

Other computerization projects:

Technical projects online: Virtual tour
How accessed: Palace & Museum, main page

Notes: Bilingual English/French Web site but some information available only in French. Four databases freely available but only on request. Online selected works, choice of four geographic areas accessed through Collections.

AUSTRALIAN WAR MEMORIAL, CANBERRA

URL: http://www.awm.gov.au/index_flash.asp

Database:

Databases online: Yes
Computerization statement: Yes
Search capabilities: Yes
Fields: Simple, advanced
No. of objects in collection: 4,000 art, 203,000 photos, and 3,500 films
Objects online: All
Label fields: Basic and expanded
Image available: 2 sizes
Image types: Thumbnail, medium, and large: t, m, and l

Copyright for images and texts:

Copyright statement: Yes

Education:

Educational information: Yes

Access and links on-site

How accessed: Main page
Site map: Yes
Bibliography: Yes, daily update
Links: Yes, external
Archive material: Yes

Other computerization projects:

Technical projects online: Virtual tour
How accessed: About the Memorial

Notes: Five collections online; each one has simple and advanced searches plus related subjects. Access also to 350 sound recordings and 8,200 private record collections. Possibility to Log in and Save searches for later use with a Work area into which records and images may be saved for later research and image ordering. Separate Research center online

BRITISH MUSEUM, LONDON

URL: http://www.thebritishmuseum.ac.uk/

Database:

Databases online: Compass

Computerization statement: Yes
Search capabilities: Yes
Fields: Simple, directed
No. of objects in collection: 4,000 objects
Objects online: 4,000, expanding
Label fields: Basic, expanded, full
Image available: Several
Image types: Thumbnail, medium, large: t, m, l, other views

Copyright for images and texts:

Copyright statement: Yes, main page and on order form

Education:

Educational information: Yes

Access and links on-site:

How accessed: Understand, main page
Site map: Yes
Bibliography: Yes, online
Links: Yes, internal
Archive material: Yes

Other computerization projects:

Technical projects online: Online learning—two projects
How accessed: Understand, main page; Compass also have own tours.

Notes: Computers containing Compass at different points in museum and reading room. New children's Compass site. Museum has list of other tours available, including past and present exhibitions. Activities available for children in museum using Compass database. Text only option for visually impaired and for those using special screen reading software.

BRITISH LIBRARY, LONDON

URL: http://www.bl.uk/

Database:

Databases online: Yes
Computerization statement: Yes
Search capabilities: Yes
Fields: Guided search
No. of objects in collection: Not listed, different collections
Objects online: Different collections
Label fields: Basic and expanded
Image available: 3 sizes
Image types: Thumbnail, medium, and large: t, 41kb, 234 KB

Copyright for images and texts:

Copyright statement: Yes

Education:

Educational information: Yes

Access and links on-site:

How accessed: Collections, main page
Site map: Yes
Bibliography: Yes
Links: Yes
Archive material: Yes

Other computerization projects:

Technical projects online: Digitization turning the pages; information only
How accessed: About Us & Collections

Note: Various online research resources available.

LACMA LOS ANGELES COUNTY MUSEUM OF ART, LOS ANGELES

URL: http://www.lacma.org/lacma.asp

Database:

Databases online: Yes
Computerization statement: Yes
Search capabilities: Yes
Fields: Simple advanced, by department
No. of objects in collection: 100,000
Objects online: 42,562
Label fields: Basic, full
Image available: 2 sizes
Image types: Thumbnail, medium, large: t, m, and other

Copyright for images and texts:

Copyright statement: Yes

Education:

Educational information: Yes

Access and links on-site:

How accessed: Browse collections, main page under heading: Art
Site map: Yes
Bibliography: N/A
Links: Yes
Archive material: Yes

Other computerization projects:

Technical projects online: Education department project
How accessed: Main page

Notes: Search possibilities could be by department and all museum records with or without images. Includes searchable storeroom treasures, recent acquisitions. Contains information on provenance

TATE GALLERY, LONDON

URL: http://www.tate.org.uk/home/default.htm

Database:

Databases online: Yes
Computerization statement: Yes
Search capabilities: Yes
Fields: Simple, subject, artist, and simple advanced
No. of objects in collection: 50,000
Objects online: 50,000 objects, 11,000 images
Label fields: Basic, full
Image available: Several
Image types: Thumbnail, medium, and large: t, m, and l

Copyright for images and texts:

Copyright statement: Yes

Education:

Educational information: Yes

Access and links on-site:

How accessed: Link through Tate Britain, Public Programs
Site map: Yes
Bibliography: Yes
Links: Yes
Archive material: Yes

Other computerization projects:

Technical projects online: Tate Art Projects On Line; others include Online tour: Turner; interactive tour of the Gallery; Explore Tate Britain
How accessed: Highlights separate heading main page

Notes: New Research center opened April 2002 for reference and by appointment; only e-mail enquiries accepted.

NATIONAL GALLERY, LONDON

URL: http://www.nationalgallery.org.uk/

Database:

Databases online: Yes
Computerization statement: Yes
Search capabilities: Yes
Fields: Choice of options
No. of objects in collection: 2,300+
Objects online: 2,300+
Label fields: Detailed description
Image available: Various
Image types: Thumbnail, medium, and large: t, l, and selected views, reverse, etc.

Copyright for images and texts:

Copyright statement: Yes

Education:

Educational information: Yes

Access and links on-site:

How accessed: Collections, main page
Site map: Yes
Bibliography: Yes
Links: Yes
Archive material: Yes

Other computerization projects:

Technical projects online: Collection Explorer
How accessed: Collections then submenu

Notes: EuroGallery search option online with link to participating museums to browse collections, print out material, and undertake research.

GETTY, LOS ANGELES

URL: http://www.getty.edu/

Database:

Databases online: Yes
Computerization statement: N/A
Search capabilities: Yes
Fields: Choice of options
No. of objects in collection: 2,000,000 photo study collection
Objects online: N/A
Label fields: Basic, detailed with links
Image available: Several
Image types: Thumbnail, medium, large: t, m, l, zoom

Copyright for images and texts:
Copyright statement: N/A

Education:
Educational information: Yes

Access and links on-site:
How accessed: Main page
Site map: Yes
Bibliography: Research tools link
Links: Yes
Archive material: Yes

Other computerization projects:
Technical projects online: Video of the Day
How accessed: Main page, also linked through Collections

Note: Research Tools offer a wide range of digital library and other resources, including online databases.

FAMSF FINE ARTS MUSEUM, SAN FRANCISCO

URL: http://www.thinker.org/

Database:

Databases online: Yes, access by Thinker Image Base
Computerization statement: Yes
Search capabilities: Yes
Fields: Keywords + advanced
No. of objects in collection: 82,000+
Objects online: 82,000 images
Label fields: basic + links through related key words
Image available: 3 sizes
Image types: Thumbnail, medium, large: t, m, zoom

Copyright for images and texts:
Copyright statement: Yes

Education:
Educational information: Yes

Access and links on-site:
How accessed: Main page
Site map: N/A
Bibliography: No
Links: Yes
Archive material: No

Other computerization projects:

Technical projects online: Virtual Gallery—create your own images
How accessed: Image Base link

Note: Comprises the Legion of Honor Museum and de Young Museum (at present closed until 2005).

METROPOLITAN MUSEUM, NEW YORK

URL: http://www.metmuseum.org/

Database:

Databases online: Yes
Computerization statement: Yes
Search capabilities: Yes
Fields: Artist, period, style, keyword
No. of objects in collection: 3,000,000
Objects online: 3,500 + other options available from different departments
Label fields: Basic, full
Image available: Several
Image types: Thumbnail, medium, and large: small t, m, l, and zoom, various others

Copyright for images and texts:

Copyright statement: Yes

Education:

Educational information: Yes

Access and links on-site:

How accessed: Main page
Site map: Yes
Bibliography: Internal link
Links: Yes
Archive material: Yes

Other computerization projects:

Technical projects online: Several—Timeline of Art history
How accessed: Main page

Note: Provenance research project providing information online.

BRITISH GOVERNMENT ART COLLECTION, LONDON

URL: http://www.gac.culture.gov.uk/home/index.asp

Database:

Databases online: Yes
Computerization statement: Yes

Search capabilities: Yes
Fields: Artist, work of art, periods + subcategories
No. of objects in collection: 12,000+
Objects online: 4,000
Label fields: Basic, expanded
Image available: 2 sizes
Image types: Thumbnail, medium, and large: t, m

Copyright for images and texts:

Copyright statement: Yes

Education:

Educational information: No

Access and links on-site:

How accessed: Main page
Site map: No
Bibliography: No
Links: No
Archive material: No

Other computerization projects:

Technical projects online: None
How accessed: N/A

Notes: Explanation of database entries. Consists of works of art, paintings, drawings, sculptures, textiles displayed in British buildings throughout the world, and Provenance research online.

NATIONAL GALLERY OF ART, WASHINGTON

URL: http://www.nga.gov/

Database:

Databases online: Yes
Computerization statement: Yes
Search capabilities: Yes
Fields: Artist, title, + combination
No. of objects in collection: 100,000
Objects online: 5,100 images, text data 100,000 objects
Label fields: Basic, full
Image available: Several
Image types: Thumbnail, medium, and large: several

Copyright for images and texts:

Copyright statement: Yes

Education:

Educational information: Yes

Access and links on-site:

How accessed: Main page
Site map: Yes
Bibliography: Yes
Links: Yes
Archive material: Yes

Other computerization projects:

Technical projects online: Overviews, web tours, and virtual tours
How accessed: Main page

Notes: Bibliography, exhibition history, location, provenance, and conservation notes.

SMITHSONIAN AMERICAN ART MUSEUM, WASHINGTON

URL: http://www.nmaa.si.edu/

Database:

Databases online: Yes, several separately accessed
Computerization statement: Various
Search capabilities: Yes
Fields: Simple, directed
No. of objects in collection: N/A
Objects online: 8,400
Label fields: Basic
Image available: 2 sizes
Image types: Thumbnail, medium, and large: t, m

Copyright for images and texts:

Copyright statement: Yes

Education:

Educational information: Yes

Access and links on-site:

How accessed: Main page
Site map: Yes
Bibliography: Yes
Links: Yes
Archive material: Yes

Other computerization projects:

Technical projects online: American Art Virtual classroom
How accessed: Education

Notes: Link available via Art inventories, main page to American Art in collections worldwide database http://www.siris.si.edu/.

THE ART INSTITUTE OF CHICAGO, CHICAGO

URL: http://www.artic.edu/aic/

Database:

Databases online: Yes
Computerization statement: Yes
Search capabilities: Yes
Fields: Search by topic
No. of objects in collection: Each department lists their own number of objects.
Objects online: Not listed
Label fields: Basic, full
Image available: 3 sizes
Image types: Thumbnail, medium, and large: t, m, and l

Copyright for images and texts:

Copyright statement: Yes

Education:

Educational information: Yes

Access and links on-site:

How accessed: Collections
Site map: Yes
Bibliography: Yes
Links: Yes
Archive material: Yes

Other computerization projects:

Technical projects online: Several. See list in Notes. Includes Explore the Galleries, QuickTime.
How accessed: Collections, then submenu

Notes: Various technical projects online include Play—games about art; Discover—exhibitions; Explore—galleries; Read—publications

An Example of a Digitized Collection

DIVISION OF ANTHROPOLOGY, AMERICAN MUSEUM OF NATURAL HISTORY

This site gives researchers all over the world a powerful tool to study the North American, Pacific, African, and Asian Ethnographic Collections maintained in the museum (about 130,000 artifacts with their images are online). ColdFusion is used to implement direct access to the relational database. *Contact: Nina Gregorev* grigri@amnh.org

FIGURE IX.1   Object from the online site of the American Museum of Natural History (http://www.amnh.org)

POTTERY BOWL, DECORATED [H/15170]
Culture: HOPI (MOKI)
Locale: AZ, NAVAJO COUNTY, HOPI INDIAN RESERVATION, FIRST MESA VICINITY
Country: USA
Material: CLAY, PIGMENT
Dimensions: D:17.7 H:9 RIM:16.7
Donor: HRDLICKA, ALES, DR. Accession No: 1900-51

Digitization Guidelines: A Selected List

SELECTION CRITERIA OF MINERVA EUROPE AT HTTP:// WWW.MINERVAEUROPE.ORG/GUIDELINES.HTM

The list is not exhaustive but is selective. The list is limited to guidelines for digitization of paper based on documentary heritage, which includes manuscripts, printed books, and photographs of libraries, archives, and museums, not for digitization of multimedia materials. Toolbox and tutorials have been included as well, as these learning resources are valuable as guidelines.

The selected guidelines have been produced by public and private institutions. Some are for guiding the digitization projects; others are related to digitization programs where the guidelines want to reach the strategy and mission of single institutions. The criteria followed for inclusion was that of general interest for professionals worldwide.

The list of digitization guidelines is a work in progress, to be updated constantly. The data chosen for description are Author, Contributor (if existing), Title, Description, Date, Format, and URL. The presentation is in alphabetical order by author. We welcome your comments and suggestions.

- **AHDS (Arts and Humanities Data Service)**

  GUIDE TO GOOD PRACTICE IN THE CREATION AND USE OF DIGITAL RESOURCES

  Available formats: HTML

  http://www.ahds.ac.uk/guides/index.htm

  Guidelines for Archaeology, History, Performing Arts, Textual Studies, Visual Arts. Each of these guides includes tips for discovering and reusing digital data, information about creating and managing new digital data, and guidance to ensure proper preparation and documentation of these data for long-term archiving

  MANAGING DIGITAL COLLECTIONS

  Available formats: HTML

  http://ahds.ac.uk/managing.htm

This guide gives a framework of strategies and standards for developing, managing, and distributing high-quality digital collections.

- **British Library**

  OBJECTIVES OF DIGITIZATION

  Available formats: HTML

  http://www.bl.uk/about/policies/digital.html#one

  The policy covers all materials originally produced in nondigital form (e.g., printed matter of all kinds, manuscripts, photographs, drawings, paintings, sound recordings, microforms), the digitization of which would fulfill one or more of the desired objectives. It includes objectives, scope, context, and BL examples.

  PRESERVATION AND DIGITIZATION: PRINCIPLES, PRACTICES, AND POLICIES

  Available formats: HTML; PDF; print publication

  http://www.bl.uk/services/preservation/freeandpaid.html

  Realized by NPO (National Preservation Office), this is a series of guidelines whose aim is to provide an independent focus for ensuring the preservation and continued accessibility of library and archive material. Free and paid material is offered.

- **CHIN (Canadian Heritage Information Network)**

  CREATING AND MANAGING DIGITAL CONTENT (April 2002)

  Available formats: HTML

  http://www.chin.gc.ca/English/Digital_Content/Capture_Collections/index.html

  Series of Guidelines for creating and maintaining a digitization project. The titles include:

  Capture your collections

  Web site development

  Web site development resources

  Intellectual property

  Collection management

  Standards

  PRODUCING ONLINE HERITAGE PROJECTS (August 2002)

  Available formats: HTML

  http://www.chin.gc.ca/English/Digital_Content/Producing_Heritage/index.html

  This handbook is for heritage professionals who are developing online content, and helps them to achieve the benefits available from web-based education and promotion. It focuses on skills needed for the creation, management, and presentation of digital content. The index includes:

  Project planning

  Project development

  Getting ready to launch

  Product maintenance

  Annexes: Glossary, Bibliography, Project manager's tools and templates.

PROGRAM GUIDELINES (April 2002)

Available formats: HTML; PDF

http://www.chin.gc.ca/English/Members/Vmc_Investment_Program/
   guidelines.html

Virtual Museums of Canada Investment Program. It includes:

Operating principles

Performance indicators

Governance structures

Content policy

Skills development

Annexes: Guidelines for calculating cost/values.

CAPTURE YOUR COLLECTIONS. PLANNING AND IMPLEMENTING
DIGITIZATION PROJECTS (April 2002)

Available formats: HTML; PDF

http://www.chin.gc.ca/English/Digital_Content/ Managers_Guide/index.html

Modules and sections of an online course on digitization. It includes:

Project planning

Legal Issues related to digitization

Determining the costs of a digitization project

Standards and guidelines to consider

Implementation

Maintenance/management

- **CLIR (Council on Libraries and Information Resources)**

  Abby Smith. BUILDING AND SUSTAINING DIGITAL COLLECTIONS:
  MODELS FOR LIBRARIES AND ARCHIVES (August 2001)

  Available formats: HTML; print publication

  http://www.clir.org/pubs/abstract/pub100abst.html

  This guide brings together libraries, museums, and academic communities. The
     focus is on scholarly publishing, with presentations of business models. This is
     an agenda for:

  Develop sound selection criteria

  Identify online audience

  Manage intellectual property rights

  Develop and share best practices for technological issues

  Implement cost recovery strategy

  Manage the institutional transformation

- **Colorado Digitization Project**

  DIGITAL TOOLBOX (2002-2003)

  Available formats: HTML

  http://www.cdpheritage.org/resource/toolbox/index.html

  The purpose of this toolbox is to introduce cultural heritage institutions to the
     range of issues associated with digitization of primary source materials. Provides
     links to general resources, bibliographies, initiatives, and clearinghouses on
     selection, scanning, quality control, metadata creation, and other project man-
     agement issues. Also offers a glossary of digital imaging terms.

- **Cornell University Library**

  MOVING THEORY INTO PRACTICE: DIGITAL IMAGING TUTORIAL (2002–2003)

  Available formats: HTML; PDF
  http://www.library.cornell.edu/preservation/tutorial/contents.html
  This tutorial, produced also in Spanish and French, includes:
  Basic terminology
  Selection
  Conversion
  Quality control
  Metadata
  Technical Infrastructure
  Digitization chain
  Image creation
  File Management
  Delivery
  Presentation
  Digital Preservation
  Management
  Continuing Education

- **CUL (Columbia University Libraries)**

  Anne R. Kenney, Stephen Chapman. DIGITAL IMAGING FOR LIBRARIES AND ARCHIVES

  Available formats: HTML; print publication
  http://www.library.cornell.edu/preservation/dila.html
  The volume begins with a theoretical overview of the key concepts, vocabulary, and challenges associated with digital conversion of paper- and film-based materials. This is followed by an overview of the hardware/software, communications, and managerial considerations associated with implementing a technical infrastructure to support a full imaging program. Additional chapters present information on the creation of databases and indexes, the implications of outsourcing imaging services, converting photographs and film intermediates, issues associated with providing long-term access to digital information, and suggestions for continuing education.

  SELECTION CRITERIA FOR DIGITAL IMAGING PROJECTS (January 2001)

  Available formats: HTML
  http://www.columbia.edu/cu/libraries/digital/criteria.html
  The criteria listed are important to assure that issues of technical feasibility, intellectual property rights, and institutional support are considered along with the value of the materials and the interest of their content.

  TECHNICAL RECOMMENDATIONS FOR DIGITAL IMAGING PROJECTS (1997)

  Available formats: HTML
  http://www.columbia.edu/acis/dl/imagespec.html

Prepared by the Image Quality Working Group of ArchivesCom, a joint Libraries/AcIS committee. This document provides recommendations for image quality, file formats, and other capture and storage issues when converting paper, photographic, and other physical materials into digital form.

GUIDELINES FOR PROVIDING ACCESS TO DIGITAL IMAGES (2001)
Available formats: HTML
http://www.columbia.edu/cu/lweb/projects/digital/policy.html
Access to digital images should be provided in the most open level, consistent with the protection of intellectual property rights, and compliant with the local policies on the exercise of such rights.

- **DLF (Digital Library Federation)**

DIGITAL LIBRARY STANDARDS AND PRACTICES (October 2002. Last revision)
Available formats: HTML
http://www.diglib.org/standards.htm
The DLF documents and promotes adoption of standards and best practices that support the effective acquisition, interchange, persistence, and assessment of digital library collections and services.

GUIDES TO QUALITY IN VISUAL RESOURCE IMAGING (July 2000)
Available formats: HTML
http://www.rlg.org/visguides/
This guide includes:
Introduction
Planning an Imaging Project, by Linda Serenson Colet
Selecting a Scanner, by Don Williams
Imaging Systems: the Range of Factors Affecting Image Quality, by Donald D'Amato
Measuring Quality of Digital Masters, by Franziska Frey
File Formats for Digital Masters, by Franziska Frey

- **DLM Forum**

GUIDELINES ON BEST PRACTICES FOR USING ELECTRONIC INFORMATION: HOW TO DEAL WITH MACHINE READABLE DATA AND ELECTRONIC DOCUMENTS (1996 first edition; 1997, updated and enlarged edition)
Available formats: HTML
http://europa.eu.int/ISPO/dlm/documents/guidelines.html
The DLM Forum, organized jointly by the Member States of the European Union and the European Commission in Brussels in December 1996, brought together experts from industry, research, administration, and archives to discuss a topic of ever increasing importance: the memory of the information society.
The Guidelines include:
From data to structured electronic information
Information life cycle and allocation of responsibilities

Design, creation, and maintenance of electronic information
Short- and long-term preservation of electronic information
Accessing and disseminating information
Annexes: Terminology, Checklist for electronic information strategy, How to
select metadata, Standards.

- **eLib**

  PRESERVATION STUDIES (SUPPORTING STUDIES) (1998–2000)

  http://www.ukoln.ac.uk/services/elib/papers/supporting/
  Managed by the British Library Research and Innovation Centre, the series Preservation Studies offer several reports on creating and preserving digital image
  collections. One of the goals is to compare various digital preservation strategies
  for different data types and formats. Studies included are:

  John Bennett. A FRAMEWORK OF DATA TYPES AND FORMATS, AND
  ISSUES AFFECTING THE LONG TERM PRESERVATION OF DIGITAL
  MATERIAL
  Available formats: HTML; PDF
  Monika Blake, David Haynes, Tanya Jowett, and David Streatfield. RESPONSI-
  BILITY FOR DIGITAL ARCHIVING AND LONG TERM ACCESS TO
  DIGITAL DATA
  Available formats: HTML; PDF
  Seamus Ross and Ann Gow. DIGITAL ARCHAEOLOGY: RESCUING
  NEGLECTED AND DAMAGED DATA RESOURCES
  Available formats: Executive summary: PDF; Full Study: PDF (Mounted Novem-
  ber 15, 1999)
  Alan Poulter. PRESERVATION OF DIGITAL MATERIALS; POLICY AND
  STRATEGY ISSUES FOR THE UK
  Available formats: HTML
  Denise Lievesley and Simon Jones. AN INVESTIGATION INTO THE DIGI-
  TAL PRESERVATION NEEDS OF UNIVERSITIES AND RESEARCH
  FUNDERS
  Available formats: HTML (mounted November 11, 1998)
  Neil Beagrie and Dan Greenstein. A STRATEGIC POLICY FRAMEWORK
  FOR CREATING AND PRESERVING DIGITAL COLLECTIONS
  Available formats: HTML; PDF; RTF
  Tony Hendley. COMPARISON OF METHODS OF DIGITAL
  PRESERVATION
  Available formats: PDF; HTML; RTF

- **The Getty Trust**

  LEARN ABOUT THE GETTY VOCABULARIES

  Available formats: HTML
  http://www.getty.edu/research/conducting_research/vocabularies/
  The vocabularies contain terms, names, and other information about people, pla-
  ces, things, and concepts relating to art, architecture, and material culture.
  Murtha Baca. INTRODUCTION TO METADATA: PATHWAYS TO DIGI-
  TAL INFORMATION (May 2000)

Available formats: HTML; PDF; print publication
http://www.getty.edu/research/conducting_research/standards/intrometadata/
Version 2 of the guide, which, rather than including a single crosswalk as in the
    previous version, is now offering a "suite" of metadata crosswalks that map dif-
    ferent sets of metadata. The author will continue to add to and revise this sec-
    tion as developments arise in the development of metadata schemas that are still
    evolving (e.g., Dublin Core Qualified, VRA Core 3.0).

- **HATII (Humanities Advanced Technology and Information Institute) and
  NINCH (National Initiative for a Networked Cultural Heritage)**

  THE NINCH GUIDE TO GOOD PRACTICE IN THE DIGITAL
  REPRESENTATION & MANAGEMENT OF CULTURAL HERITAGE
  MATERIALS (October 2002—Version 1.0 First edition)

  Available formats: HTML
  http://www.nyu.edu/its/humanities/ninchguide/
  The Guide describes the process of creating and distributing digital collections
      and looks at mechanisms by which the institution that created or holds digital
      collections can manage them to maximum advantage. It includes:
  Project planning
  Selecting materials
  Rights management
  Digitization and encoding of text
  Capture and management of images
  Audio/video capture and management
  Quality control and assurance
  Working with others
  Distribution
  Assessment of projects by user evaluation
  Digital asset management
  Preservation
  In Appendixes: Equipment, Metadata, Digital Data Capture: Sampling

- **Harvard University Library**

  SELECTION FOR DIGITIZATION: A DECISION MAKING MATRIX
  (December 1997)

  Available formats: HTML; PDF
  http://www.clir.org/pubs/reports/hazen/matrix.html
  A decision-making matrix, produced for guiding professionals in the selection. It
      is included in the Harvard program: Library preservation resources principles
      and guides.

- **IMLS (Institute of Museum and Library Services)**

  A FRAMEWORK OF GUIDANCE FOR BUILDING GOOD DIGITAL
  COLLECTIONS (November 2001)

  Available formats: HTML
  http://www.imls.gov/pubs/forumframework.htm

Indicators are listed for digital objects, metadata, collections and projects, within the context of networked services. Report of the IMLS Digital Library Forum on the National Science Digital Library Program.
Reference in: Priscilla Caplan et al. (2001):
http://www.imls.gov/pubs/forumframework.htm

- **Library of Congress**

DIGITAL STRATEGY FOR THE LIBRARY OF CONGRESS (2000)

Available formats: HTML; print publication; e-book
http://www.nap.edu/catalog/9940.html
LC21: A Digital Strategy for the Library of Congress discusses challenges and provides recommendations for moving forward at the Library of Congress. Topics covered include:
Digital collections
Digital preservation
Digital cataloging (metadata)
Strategic planning
Human resources
General management
Budgetary issues

CHALLENGES TO BUILDING AN EFFECTIVE DIGITAL LIBRARY

Available formats: HTML
http://memory.loc.gov/ammem/dli2/html/cbedl.html
The staff of the NDLP (National Digital Library Program) at the Library of Congress have identified ten challenges that must be met if large and effective digital libraries are to be created during the twenty-first century. The challenges are grouped under the following broad categories:
Building the resource
Interoperability
Intellectual property
Providing effective access
Sustaining the resource

TECHNICAL NOTES BY TYPE OF MATERIAL

Available formats: HTML
http://memory.loc.gov/ammem/dli2/html/document.html
The notes provide general comments on digital reproductions of textual materials for American Memory, including:
Searchable text
Textual material available for use in DLI-Phase II
Challenges faced by NDLP (National Digital Library Program)

BACKGROUND PAPERS AND TECHNICAL INFORMATION

Available formats: HTML
http://memory.loc.gov/ammem/ftpfile.html
These versions represent the final document of NDL Requests for Proposals for scanning and text conversion services. Contracts have been awarded for the work described in the Requests for Proposals.

MANUSCRIPT DIGITIZATION DEMONSTRATION PROJECT. FINAL
REPORT (October 1998)
Available formats: HTML
http://memory.loc.gov/ammem/pictel/
The Manuscript Digitization Demonstration Project was sponsored by the
Library of Congress Preservation Directorate and was carried out in coopera-
tion with the NDLP from 1994 to 1997. The questions framed are:
What type of image is best suited for the digitization of large manuscript collec-
tions, especially collections consisting mostly of twentieth-century typescripts?
What level of quality strikes the best balance between production economics and
the requirements set by future uses of the images?
Will the same type of image that offers high-quality reformatting also provide efficient online access for researchers?

LESSONS LEARNED: NATIONAL DIGITAL LIBRARY COMPETITION
(January 2001)
Available formats: HTML
http://lcweb2.loc.gov/ammem/award/lessons/lessons.html
LC/Ameritech award winners are learning many lessons about digitization proj-
ects in the implementation of their award. To help award winners, digital project
managers, and others interested in this emerging field, the competition staff has
summarized, extracted, and paraphrased points from some of the interim reports
submitted by awardees. These include:
Formats and specifications for digital reproductions
Production work flow and project management
Intellectual access

CONSERVATION IMPLICATIONS OF DIGITIZATION PROJECTS
Available formats: HTML
http://memory.loc.gov/ammem/techdocs/conservation.html
This paper was written by a group of Library of Congress conservators who have
worked closely with NDLP digitization projects and NDLP project leaders
since the beginning of the program in 1995. The multifaceted and precedent
setting role which conservation plays in digital image conversion projects in the
NDLP in the areas of consultation, training, and treatment for scanning is
discussed.

- **NARA (National Archives and Records Administration)**

Steven Puglia. GUIDELINES FOR DIGITIZING ARCHIVAL MATERIALS
FOR ELECTRONIC ACCESS (January 1998)
Available formats: PDF
http://www.archives.gov/research_room/arc/arc_info
/guidelines_for_digitizing_archival_materials.pdf
These guidelines have been realized to provide a method for evaluating quality of
images produced, to estimate the data storage for access files (online) and master
files (off line), and to assist in determining upgrades of NARA infrastructure.
Differences in document type dictate differences in approach to scanning; specifications are given for textual documents, photographs, maps, plans, and over-
sized records, graphic records.

- **National Library of Australia**

  DIGITIZATION OF TRADITIONAL FORMAT LIBRARY MATERIALS. STANDARDS AND GUIDELINES

  Available formats: HTML

  http://www.nla.gov.au/digital/standards.html

  These guidelines, created for National Library staff, provide advice on digitization projects. They focus on creating digital images and displaying them on the Web, including metadata and preservation issues.

  PRESERVING ACCESS TO DIGITAL INFORMATION (PADI)

  Available formats: HTML

  http://www.nla.gov.au/padi/

  The PADI site offers a subject gateway to digital preservation resources. Includes current information on digital preservation-related events, organizations, policies, strategies, and guidelines. Also includes glossaries of terms that are relevant to digital information.

- **NEDCC (Northeast Document Conservation Center)**

  Maxine Sitts. HANDBOOK FOR DIGITAL PROJECTS: A MANAGEMENT TOOL FOR PRESERVATION AND ACCESS (December 2000)

  Available formats: PDF; print publication

  http://www.nedcc.org/digital/dman2.pdf

  Web resource providing information on the issues surrounding the digital conversion of collection materials. With contributions from many of the School for Scanning series presenters, it provides information on project selection and management, technical and copyright considerations, and digital longevity and includes commentary on the transformation in scholarly access and preservation tenets required to fully utilize and maintain digital images. Given at NEDCC's school for scanning conferences, Andover, MA. It includes:

  Rationale for digitization and preservation

  Considerations for project management

  Selection of materials for scanning

  Overview of copyright issues

  Technical primer

  Developing best practices: guidelines from case studies

  Vendor relations

  Digital longevity

  Scholar commentary.

- **NINCH (National Initiative for a Networked Cultural Heritage)**

  see HATII

- **Nordinfo. NDLC**

  GUIDELINES ON THE ESTABLISHMENT OF DIGITIZATION SERVICES (July 1997/updated November 2000)

  Available formats: HTML

  http://www.nordinfo.helsinki.fi/publications/nordnytt/ nnytt3-4_97/solbakk.htm

It includes:
Digitizing documents where the original is on paper or film base
Digitizing audio
Digitizing video

- **NSDL/SMETE (Science Mathematics Engineering and Technology Education)**

NSDL METADATA PRIMER (Last revision January 2003)

Available formats: HTML

http://metamanagement.comm.nsdlib.org/outline.html
The National SMET (Science, Mathematics, Engineering and Technology Education) Digital Library (NSDL) is being constructed to support excellence in SMET for all Americans. NSDL is a comprehensive information system built as a distributed network and will develop and make accessible high quality collections. Reference: C. Manduca, F. McMartin, and D. Mogk, "Pathways to progress: vision and plans for developing the NSDL" (2001):
http://doclib.comm.nsdlib.org/PathwaysToProgress.pdf. This primer is intended to serve NSDL partners and collaborators as they work with NSDL staff to make their metadata available through the NSDL Metadata Repository. Its primary clientele are those NSDL-funded projects which are at the beginning stages of awareness and use of metadata, but there are also sections that will be useful to others.

NSDL BUILDING COLLECTIONS (October 2002)
Available formats: HTML
http://collections.comm.nsdlib.org/cgi-in/wiki.pl? Building Collections
Checklist, tools, and examples are provided for those wanting to contribute to build the NSDL collection, but it is useful also to others.

- **RLG (Research Libraries Group)**

RLG GUIDELINES FOR MICROFILMING TO SUPPORT
DIGITIZATION (February 2003)

Available formats: HTML
http://www.rlg.org/preserv/
Offers supporting materials to institutions in their efforts to preserve and improve access to endangered research materials.

RLG TOOLS FOR DIGITAL IMAGING (May 2002)
Available formats: HTML
http://www.rlg.org/preserv/RLGtools.html
The tools include worksheets and guidelines for creating digital imaging services. The following documents are available:
The RLG Worksheet for Estimating Digital Reformatting Costs
The RLG Guidelines for Creating a Request for Proposal for Digital Imaging Services
The RLG Model Request for Information (RFP)
The RLG Model Request for Proposals (RFP)
Reference: Papers given at the RLG and NPO Preservation Conference
Guidelines for Digital Imaging (1998): http://www.rlg.org/preserv/joint/

RLG PRESERVING DIGITAL INFORMATION (August 2002)

Available formats: HTML; PDF

http://www.rlg.org/ArchTF/

The Commission on Preservation and Access (CPA) and RLG formed the Task Force on Archiving of Digital Information, charged with investigating and recommending means to ensure "continued access indefinitely into the future of records stored in digital electronic form." The report is an outcome of the Task Force.

Anne R. Kenny and Oya Y. Rieger. RLG MOVING THEORY INTO PRACTICE (May 2001)

Available formats: HTML; print publication

http://www.rlg.org/preserv/mtip2000.html

The book advocates an integrated approach to digital imaging programs, from selection to access to preservation, with a heavy emphasis on the intersection of institutional, cultural objectives, and practical digital applications.

- **TASI (Technical Advisory Service for Images)**

MANAGING DIGITIZATION PROJECTS (2002)

Available formats: HTML; printed pack

http://www.tasi.ac.uk/advice/managing/jidi_workflow.html

Funded by the Joint Information Systems Committee (UK), provides information on creating, storing, and delivering digital image collections. The course includes:

Deciding to digitize

Managing the work flow

Managing the project

Looking after copyright, IPR, ethics, and data protection

Project management

Work flow guidelines

Why "Archive Standard"?

Copyright

Coping with copyright

Quick reference copyright guide

Example license agreement

JIDI digitization model

Lessons learned from the JIDI project

Risk assessment

Staff training

Also lists events and information resources of interest to those involved in digital imaging initiatives.

- **TEI (Text Encoding Initiative)**

C.M. Sperberg-Mc Queen and Lou Bernard. GUIDELINES FOR ELECTRONIC TEXT ENCODING AND

INTERCHANGE (March 2002—P4 Edition)

Available formats: XML

http://www.tei-c.org/P4X/

A new and corrected version of the TEI Guidelines, XML-compatible, edited by the TEI Consortium (The Association for Computers and the Humanities

(ACH), The Association for Computational Linguistics (ACL), and The Association for Literary and Linguistic Computing (ALLC). The Guidelines provide means of representing those features of a text which need to be identified explicitly, in order to facilitate processing of the text by computer programs. In particular, they specify a set of markers (or tags) that may be inserted in the electronic representation of the text, in order to mark the text structure and other textual features of interest.

- **UNESCO/ICA/IFLA**

  GUIDELINES FOR DIGITIZATION PROJECTS FOR COLLECTION AND HOLDINGS IN THE PUBLIC DOMAIN, PARTICULARLY THOSE HELD BY LIBRARIES AND ARCHIVES (March 2002)
  Available formats: PDF
  http://www.ifla.org/VII/s19/pubs/digit-guide.pdf
  Guidelines for digitalization/digitization projects, including planning and setting up projects, selection, management, and production processes. They deal with paper material, manuscripts, printed books, and photographs. They are not concerned with digitization programs as an integral part of an institution strategy. They include checklists for each chapter.

- **University of California Los Angeles UCLA**

  Kim Thompson. DIGITAL PROJECTS GUIDELINES AND STANDARD (1998)
  Available formats: HTML
  http://www.library.ucsb.edu/ucpag/digselec.html
  The list of criteria is recommended to guide collection development librarians and preservation librarians in selecting collections of analogue materials (including paper, film, audio, and video) for conversion to digital format. Some of the criteria are based on conventional selection and preservation considerations common to all formats; others arise from the opportunities and constraints unique to digital technologies.

- **University of Virginia Library. Electronic Text Center**

  ARCHIVAL DIGITAL IMAGE CREATION (1996–1997)
  Available formats: HTML
  http://etext.lib.virginia.edu/helpsheets/scanimage.html
  Basic Helpsheets for helping to making decisions. They include:
  Text Scanning: A Basic Helpsheet
  Image Scanning: A Basic Helpsheet
  The Special Collections Department

Glossary

Accession number—Registrar number used in a museum.

ASCII—American Standard Code for Information Interchange, set of codes used to represent letters, numbers, a few symbols, and control characters. Originally designed for teletype operations, it has found wide application in computers. A seven-digit (or seven-bit) binary number (see binary system) can represent one of 128 distinct codes. Thus, in decimal equivalents, the series "72, 69, 76, 76, 79" represents the letters "h, e, l, l, o" in ASCII. With the introduction of its personal computer in 1981, the International Business Machines Company (IBM) increased the number of available characters to 256 by using an eight-bit byte. This IBM-extended ASCII set has become a de facto standard. However, the inability of US-ASCII to correctly represent many other languages became an obvious and intolerable fault as computer use outside the United States and United Kingdom increased. As a consequence, national extensions to US-ASCII were developed that were incompatible with one another. This in turn led to the standardization of sixteen-bit (or "double-byte") character sets, such as Unicode, that could accommodate large numbers of languages.

Back- and front-end—Sides of a program. The back-end is not viewed by the user while the front-end is seen on the screen.

DPI—Dots per inch.

GUI—The users' instinctive use of the tools is a science based on the anatomical morphology combined with human motion.

Hyperlinks—Associated texts or images.

In-house support—Usually a "help desk" manned by computer professionals that services the computers of the company or museum.

Intranet—Internal network. Not accessible by the public from their home computers.

Legacy terms—Terms that are part of the language used by the institution.

Listserves—A list of users sharing information managed by a "list moderator." A contraction of "list service."

Media—Material or data (e.g., videos, sound tracks, catalogue images).

Off-the shelf product—A ready-made program.

Thumbnail image—Small image representing a large image, the size of your thumbnail.

Unicode—A set of codes used to represent letters, numbers, control characters, and the like, designed for use internationally in computers. Adopted as an international standard in 1992, it is intended to replace ASCII as the primary alphanumeric character set. Unicode is a "double-byte," or sixteen-digit, binary number code that can represent up to 65,536 items. The Unicode standard defines codes for letters, special characters, and other linguistic symbols used in every major language written today. It includes the Latin alphabet used for English; the Cyrillic alphabet used for Russian; the Greek, Hebrew, and Arabic alphabets; and other alphabets and alphabet-like writing systems used in countries across Europe, Africa, the Indian subcontinent, and Asia, such as Japanese kana, Korean hangul, and Chinese bopomofo. The largest part of the Unicode standard is devoted to thousands of unified character codes for Chinese, Japanese, and Korean ideographs.

Bibliography

Agnus, Jim. "Managing Your Museum Web Site." Ed-Resources.Net. http://www.ed-resources.net/mw99/.

Alt-Soft Ltd. "Information and Communication Technologies," February 28, 2003. http://www.kamis.ru/news.

Amarc Data International. "Information about AMARC Data International." Amarc Data International Pty Ltd., 1991.

AMOL (Australian Museums and Galleries Online). "Collections Australia Network." http://amol.org.au/collection/collections_index.asp.

Arminta, Neal. *Exhibits for the Small Museum—A Handbook.* Nashville, Tennessee: American Association for State and Local History, 1976.

Art Institute of Chicago Web site. http://www.artic.edu/aic/.

Art Search. "Art and Media." http://www.artsearch.net/.

ADAM (Art, Design, Architecture and Media). "Information Gateway Quick Guide to Metadata." http://adam.ac.uk/adam/metadata.html.

Australian War Memorial. http://www.awm.gov.au.

AXS Optical Technology Resource. *ARTAccess.* Berkeley, California: AXS, 1991.

Ayres, F. H., J. Cullen, C. Gierl, J. A. W. Huggill, M. J. Ridley, and I. S. Torsun. "QUALCAT: Automation of Quality Control in Cataloguing." Final Report. Great Britain: British Library Research and Development Report, March 1991.

Baca, Murtha. "Making Sense of the Tower of Babel: A Demonstration Project in Multilingual Equivalency Work." *Terminology: International Journal of Theoretical and Applied Issues in Specialized Communication* 4, no. 1 (1997).

Baron, Robert A. "Computerized Collection Management: A Primer." *Registrar* 4, no. 2 (September 1987).

Bearman, David. "Automated Systems for Archives and Museums: Acquisition and Implementation Issues," Part 2 of *Archival Informatics Newsletter & Technical Report.* Pittsburgh, Pennsylvania: Archives & Museum Informatics, March 1988.

Bearman, David and Jennifer Trant, ed. *Museum Interactive Multimedia 1997: Cultural Heritage Systems Design and Interfaces.* Selected papers from the Fourth International Conference on Hypermedia and Interactivity in Museums (ICHIM '97).

Le Louvre, Paris, France, September 1–5, 1997. Pittsburgh, PA: Archives & Museum Informatics.

Bennet, Tony. *The Birth of the Museum, History, Theory, Politics.* London: Routledge, 1995.

Bernstein, B. *Sanctification and the Art of Silversmithing.* Judaica Museum, The Hebrew Home for the Aged at Riverdale, 1994.

Besser, Howard, "User Interfaces for Museums." School of Library & Information Science. University of Pittsburgh, 1989. http://www.gseis.ucla.edu/~howard /Papers/newpapers/MCN89.html#References.

Blanchard, Kenneth and Spencer Johnson. *The One Minute Manager.* New York: Berkley Books, 1983.

Booth, Ben and Christine J. Heap. "High Resolution Digital Image Storage at the National Railway Museum, York" In *Museums and Interactive Multimedia*, edited by Diane Lees, 1–5. Proceedings of the Sixth International Conference of the MDA and the Second International Conference on Hypermedia and Interactivity in Museums (ICHIM '93). Cambridge, England, September 20–24, 1993. Pittsburgh, Pennsylvania: Archives & Museum Informatics, 1993.

British Government Art Collection. http://www.gac.culture.gov.uk/home/index.asp.

British Library, London. http://www.bl.uk/.

British Museum, London. http://www.thebritishmuseum.ac.uk/.

Buck, Rebecca A. and Jean Allman Gilmore, eds. *The New Museum Registration Methods*, 4th ed. Washington, D.C.: American Association of Museums, 1998.

Buckley, Georgina. *Australian Visual Arts Internet Resources.* Canberra, Austraila: Australian National University Library, 1999. http://anulib.anu.edu.au/clusters/ita /subjects/austvisres.html.

Burcaw, G. Ellis. *Introduction to Museum Work.* Nashville, Tennessee: American Association for State and Local History, 1975.

Carnegie Museum of Art. http://www.cmoa.org/.

Case, Mary, ed. *Registrars on Record: Essays on Museum Collections Management.* Washington, D.C.: Registrars Committee of the American Association of Museums, 1988.

Cave, Mike, Marilyn Deegan and Louise Heinink. "Copyright Clearance in the Refugee Studies Centre Digital Library Project." *RLG DigiNews* 4, no. 5 (October 15, 2000). http://www.rlg.org/preserv/diginews/diginews4-5.html.

Chapman, Stephen, Paul Conway, and Anne R. Kenney. "Digital Imaging and Preservation Microfilm: The Future of the Hybrid Approach for the Preservation of Brittle Books." *RLG DigiNews* 3, no. 1 (February 15, 1999). http://www.rlg.org /preserv/diginews/diginews3-1.html#feature1.

CHIN (Canadian Heritage Information Network). "About the CHIN's Religious Objects Database." Bilingual format, Canadian Heritage Information Network, Direction des Musées de France and Réunion des Musées Nationaux, 1994. http://www.chin.gc.ca/English/Reference_Library/Acfr/index.html.

CHIN (Canadian Heritage Information Network). http://www.chin.gc.ca/Resources /Research_Ref/Reference_Info/ACFR/e_religious_objects.html.

Christine. *Virtual Ethnography.* Thousand Oaks, California: Sage, 2000.

CIS Gallery. "Color Imaging Systems." Barneyscan Corporation, 1991.

Computer-Index of Classical Iconography: Database Samples. New Brunswick, New Jersey: Rutgers University, November 6, 1986.

Cox, J. http://www.archimuse.com.

Curits, Katherine. *Multi-Database Support for Object-Oriented, Multimedia Authoring Environments.* PhD diss., Massachusetts Institute of Technology, Department of Civil and Environmental Engineering, May 1996. https://dspace.mit.edu/handle /1721.1/7582.

Davidson Archeological Park. http://www.archpark.org.il/.

Dube, Lise Marie. *The Typologies of Cognitive Dissonance and the Self-Guided Adult Visitor: Assessing Interpretive Aids in a Fine Arts Museum.* Master's thesis, Montreal, Quebec, Concordia University, Department of Art Education, February 1998. http://www.collectionscanada.ca/obj/s4/f2/dsk1/tape10/PQDD_0003 /MQ44807.pdf.

Dudley, Dorothy H., ed. *Museum Registration Methods,* 3rd edition. Washington, D.C.: American Association of Museums, 1979.

ECMC. "Museums as Mirrors of Social Change." http://www.ecmc.de/mim/eng lish/03.html.

EMFlash. European Multimedia Forum's monthly newsletter. March 2000.

Fahy, A. *New Technologies for Museum Communication.* In *Museum, Media, Message,* edited by E. Hooper-Greenhill, 82–96. London: Routledge, 1995.

Fahy, Anne, ed. *Collection Management.* London: Routledge, 1995.

Falk, John H. and Lynn D. Dierking. *Learning from Museum's Visitors Experiences and the Making of Meaning.* Walnut Creek, California: AltaMira Press, 2000.

Falkovitch-Khain, Julia. "Trip Report of Conference." EVA 2002, Moscow, December 16, 2002.

FAMSF (Fine Arts Museum of San Francisco). http://www.thinker.org/.

Fetterman, David M. *Ethnography: Step By Step,* 2nd edition. Thousand Oaks, California: Sage, 1998.

Fisher Gallery. *The USC Interactive Art Museum at the Fisher Gallery an Art Museum for the Digital Age.* University Southern California, Los Angeles. 1998, 1999. http://digimuse.usc.edu/museum.html.

Frohne, Ursula. "Old Art and New Media: The Contemporary Museum." Afterimage (September/October1999).

GDV (Galerie Dessford Vogel). http://www.gdv.org.nz/.

Gallery Systems. "The Museum System." New York, New York: Gallery Systems, 1991. http://www.gallerysystems.com/products/tms.html.

Getty. "About the TGN and the Introduction to ULAN." http://www.getty.edu/.

Getty. *Religious Objects of the Catholic Faith, Thesaurus of Religious Objects.* Getty Institute, Canadian Heritage, Catalogo e la Documentazione ICCD book and CD ROM.

Getty. *Art & Architecture Thesaurus® Online.* http://www.getty.edu/research/conduc ting_research/vocabularies/aat/.

Getty. *ArtsEd Index.* http://www.artsednet.getty.edu/ArtsEdNet/Index/index.html.

Glaser, Jane R. with Artemis A. Zenetou. *Museums: A Place to Work: Planning Museum Careers.* London; New York: Routledge, 1996.

Greenblatt, Stephen. "Resonance and Wonder." In *Exhibiting Cultures: The Poetics and Politics of Museum Display,* edited by Ivan Karp and Steven Lavine. Washington, D.C., and London: Smithsonian Institute Press/Cambridge University Press, 1991.

Greenspun, Philip. E-mail interview by the author, November 11, 1998. In this letter Greenspun refers to his online book "Philip and Alex's Guide to Web Publishing." http://philip.greenspun.com/panda/.

Guedalia, David. Interviewed by the author, January 1999, phone conversation, Beit Shemesh, Israel.

Guedalia, Joshua. Interviewed by the author, January 2, 2003, phone conversation, Beit Shemesh, Israel.

Hannon, Hilary and Alan Tucker. *AMIS Archives and Museums Information System.* Stanford Instructional Television Network. Videorecording. Stanford, California: Research Libraries Group, 1994.

Harman, Oth. *Art Museums & Media.* Los Angeles: J. Paul Getty Trust Publications, 1994.

Hine, Christine M. *Virtual Ethnography.* Thousand Oaks, California: Sage Publications, Inc:, 2000.

Hein, Hilde. *The Exploratorium: The Museum as Laboratory.* Washington, D.C.: Smithsonian Institution Press, 1990.

Hoopes, John W. "The Future of the Past: Archaeology and Anthropology on the World Wide Web." Department of Anthropology and Museum of Anthropology, the University of Kansas. Paper prepared for the symposium *The Potential of Museum Web Sites for Research* at Museums on the Web: An International Conference, March 16–19, 1997, Los Angeles, California, http://www.ku.edu/~hoopes/mw/.

Hudon, Michele. "Multilingual Thesaurus Construction—Integrating the Views of Different Cultures in One Gateway to Knowledge and Concepts." *Information Services and Use* 17, no. 2/3 (1997): 111–123.

Hupfer, P. *The Virtual Museum: The Application of New Media in Museums.* Germany: Internationales Bauhaus-Kolloquium, 1997.

ICHIM. *Hypermedia & Interactivity in Museums.* The Proceedings of the International Conferences on Hypermedia & Interactivity in Museums (ICHIM 93-97).

Inbar, Judith. "On the History and Nature of Museums in Israel." In *The Museum and the Needs of People.* CECA Conference, Jerusalem, Israel, October 15–22, 1991.

Indiana University Art Museum. "Computerization of Art Museum Collections." http://www.iupui.edu/it/stratdir/baden.html.

Israel Museum, Jerusalem. http://www.imj.org.il/.

Jewish History Resource Center. "Museums, Exhibits and Virtual Exhibits Related to Jewish Studies." http://www.jewishhistory.huji.ac.il/links/museums.htm.

Jones, Lois Swan. *Art Information and the Internet: How to Find It, How to Use It.* Phoenix, Arizona: Oryx Press, 1999.

Joods Historisch Museum. http://www.jhm.nl/.

Keene, Suzanne. *Digital Collections, Museums and the Information Age.* Oxford, UK: Butterworth-Heinemann, 1998.

Kodak. *Technology Gets Culture: How Museums Are Using Digital Imaging.* http://webs1.kodak.com/global/en/professional/hub/museums/museums6.shtml.

Koe, Frank T. "Fabrics on File." *Museum News* (January 1990).

Koffman, Elliot B. *Pascal—A Problem Solving Approach.* Addison-Wesley microbooks popular series. Reading, Massachusetts: Addison-Wesley, 1982.

Korth, Henrey F. and Abraham Silberschatz. *Database Systems Concepts.* McGraw-Hill advanced computer science series. New York: McGraw-Hill, 1986.

Kupietzky, Allison. "Building A Bilingual Lexicon—A Case Study from the Israel Museum's Collection Database Project." In *Theme: US-Europe-Israel Cooperation in Culture X Technology,* edited by Violet Gilboa and James Hemsley, chapter 7, 1–9.

Proceedings from the EVA 2002 Harvard Symposium, Hampshire, UK: Vasari, 2002.

Larsen, Carsten U. "Collection Management: The Danish Case." *Museum* 160, no. 4 (1988): 197–199.

Lin, Dor. *The Image of the IMJ*. Survey of public opinion of The Israel Museum, Jerusalem, Summer 2000.

Linhartova, Vera. "Documentation Centre's Column: Data Bases in Japanese Art Museums." *ICOM News* 42, no. 1 (1989): 10–11.

Los Angeles County Museum of Art. http://www.lacma.org/lacma.asp.

Louvre. http://www.louvre.fr/louvrea.htm.

Ma, Xiaoyi. *Parallel Text Collections at Linguistic Data Consortium*. Linguistic Data Consortium, Philadelphia, 1999. Machine Translation Summit VII, September 13, 1999, Kent Ridge Digital Labs, National University of Singapore.

Macdonald, Sharon and Gordon Fyfe. *Theorizing the Museum: Representing Identity and Diversity in a Changing World*. Cambridge, Massachusetts: Blackwell, 1996.

MDA (Museum Documentation Association). *Terminology for Museums*. Proceedings of the International Conference held in Cambridge, England, September 21–24, 1988. Cambridge, UK: Museum Documentation Association, 1990.

MDA (Museum Documentation Association). *Software Survey—Contents General Activities Resources Events Reference*. Cambridge, UK: Museum Documentation Association, 1999.

Meles, Brigitte. "French Photographic Collections: Searching the ICONOS Database." In *Databases in the Humanities and Social Sciences-4*, edited by Lawrence J. McCrank, 449–451. Medford, New Jersey: Learned Information, 1989.

Metropolitan Museum of Art, New York. http://www.metmuseum.org/.

Mirzoeff, Nicholas, ed. *Diaspora and Visual Culture, Representing Africans and Jews*. London: Routledge, 2000.

Museum of Ethnology. http://www.ethno-museum.ac.at/.

Museum of Modern Art. *The Collection*. http://www.moma.org/.

MUVA (Museo Virtual de Artes El Pais). http://muva.elpais.com.uy/.

National Gallery of Art. http://www.nga.gov/.

National Gallery, London. http://www.nationalgallery.org.uk/.

New Museum of Contemporary Art, New York. http://www.newmuseum.org/.

Nol, Lev Yakovlevich. "Computer Literacy for Museums in the USSR." *Museum* (1989): 96–100.

Ogden Museum of Southern Art. "Tour the Ogden—Virtually." New Orleans, Louisiana, 2000. http://www.ogdenmuseum.org/tour/index.html.

Oikawa, Akifuni. "Archaeological Image Database System." International Conference on Data Bases in the Humanities and Social Sciences, Auburn University, Montgomery, Alabama, July 11, 1987.

Pearce, Susan M., ed. *Museums Objects and Collections*. London; New York: Routledge, 1992.

Pearson, Clifford A. "Exhibit Design: Breaking Out of the Display Case, Exhibits Reach Out and Touch." *Architectural Record* (September 1994): 28.

Permanent Collection of the Modern Art Museum of Fort Worth. http://www.mamfw.org/collect.htm.

Questor Systems and Malam Systems. "Questor and Malam Computerize Israel's Museums." *Museum News* 74 (March/April 1995): 66.

Questor Systems. http://www.questorsys.com.

RKD (Rijksbureau voor Kunsthistorische Documentatie—Netherlands Institute for Art History). Art & Architecture Thesaurus® translation project. The Hague, Holland. http://www.rkd.nl/frame-e.htm.

RLG (Research Libraries Group). Preserving Digital Information: Report of the Task Force on Archiving of Digital Information. http://www.rlg.org/ArchTF/.

Roberts, D. Andrew, ed. *Collections Management for Museums.* Proceedings of the International Conference, Cambridge, England, September 26–29, 1987. Cambridge, UK: Museum Documentation Association, 1988.

Rogers, Everett and F. Floyd Shoemaker. *Communication of Innovations: A Cross-Cultural Approach.* New York: Free Press. 1971.

Roth, Evan. PCs Pack as Much Computer Power as Most Museums Need. United States.

Sarasan, Lenore. "Why Museum Computer Projects Fail." *Museum News* 59 no. 4 (January/February 1981): 40–49.

Schwalbe, Kathy. *Information Technology Project Management,* 4th ed. Course Technology, Cambridge, Massachusetts, March 2005.

Schwarz, Hans-Peter, ed. *Media—Art—History Media Museum.* New York: ZKM, Center for Art & Media Karlsruhe, 1997.

Smithsonian American Art Museum. http://www.nmaa.si.edu/.

Solomon, Muriel. *Working with Difficult People.* Paramus, New Jersey: Prentice Hall Press, 2002.

Stam, Deidre C. "Public Access to Museum Information: Pressure and Policies." *Curator* 32, no. 3 (1989): 190–198.

Stam, Deidre C. "The Quest for a Code, or a Brief History of the Computerized Cataloging of Art Objects." *Art Documentation* 8 no. 1 (spring 1989): 7–15.

State Hermitage Museum Digital Collection. http://www.hermitagemuseum.org/.

Steiner, C. "Controlling Your Images (The Museum and the Licensing of Imaging Products)." *Museum News* 71, no. 4 (July 1992): 62–64.

Swan Jones, Lois. *Art Information & the Internet How to Find It, How to Use It.* Westport, Connecticut: Greenwood Publishing Group, 1998.

Tate Collections. http://www.tate.org.uk/home/default.htm.

Teather, Lynne and Kelly Wilhelm. "'Web Musing': Evaluating Museums on the Web from Learning Theory to Methodology." Paper presented at Museum and the Web, University of Toronto, Canada, 1999. http://www.archimuse.com /mw99/papers/teather/teather.html.

Thomas, Selma and Ann Mintz, eds. *The Virtual and the Real: Media in the Museum.* Washington, D.C.: American Association of Museums, 1998.

Tomislav, Sola. *Essays on Museum and their Theory—Towards a Cybernetic Museum.* Helsinki, Finland: Museums Association, 1997.

University of San Francisco. "Holocaust and Art." http://fcit.coedu.usf.edu/holocaust /arts/art.htm.

Vance, David. "The Museum Computer Network in Context." In *Museum Documentation Systems: Developments and Applications,* edited by Richard B. Light, D. Andrew Roberts, and Jennifer D. Stewart. London: Butterworths, 1986.

Vergo, Peter. *The New Museology.* London: Reaktion Books, 1989.

VADS (Visual Arts Data Service). The Surrey Institute of Art and Design at University College in Farnham, Great Britain. http://vads.ahds.ac.uk/search.html.

Wallace, Brian and Katherine Jones-Garmil. "Museums and the Internet: A Guide for the Intrepid Traveler." *Museum News* 73, no.4 (July/August 1994), 32–36, 57–62.

Watkins, Beverly T. "Computerized Catalogs Extend Access to Specialized Collections." *Chronicle of Higher Education* 38, no. 40 (June 10, 1992): A15, A17.

Wentz, Pnina."Museum Information Systems: The Case for Computerization." *The International Journal of Museum Management and Curatorship* (1989): 313–325.

Will, Leonard. "Publications on Thesaurus Construction and Use." Willpower Information: Information Management Consultants. http://www.willpower.demon.co.uk/thesbibl.htm.

Willett, Frank. "True or False? The False Dichotomy." *African Arts* 9 no. 3 (1976).

Willpower Information: Information Management Consultants. "Time Taken to Create Catalogue Records for Museum Objects." http://www.willpowerinfo.co.uk/.

Yale University Library—Virtual Exhibit. http://www.library.yale.edu/exhibition/judaica/.

Index

About the Author

DR. ALLISON SIFFRE GUEDALIA KUPIETZKY is Collections Database Manager for the Israel Museum in Jerusalem.